"If only people like these graced the covers of our news magazines, U.S. society would be a very different place. Thank you, Michael Henderson, for introducing us to sixteen heroines we might otherwise have overlooked." — **Philip Yancey**
Editor at Large, *Christianity Today*

"Michael Henderson's compelling book documents the experiences of several strong-willed women in their untiring work for peace. It is truly an inspiring book."
— **Mark O. Hatfield**
United States Senator

"It's easy to heed the trumpets of war and far harder to do the quiet, often difficult work of conflict resolution. These women have risen to the challenge to truly solve problems in their communities. Their commitment inspires us all and calls us to rededicate ourselves to peace." — **Elizabeth Furse**
United States Congresswoman

All Her Paths Are Peace

Kumarian Press Books for a World that Works

All Her Paths Are Peace:
Women Pioneers in Peacemaking
Michael Henderson

Voices from the Amazon
Binka Le Breton

The Human Farm:
A Tale of Changing Lives and Changing Lands
Katie Smith

Summer in the Balkans:
Laughter and Tears after Communism
Randall Baker

All
Her
Paths
Are
Peace

*Women Pioneers
in Peacemaking*

Michael Henderson

Kumarian Press

ALL HER PATHS ARE PEACE: *Women Pioneers in Peacemaking.*
Published 1994 in the United States of America by Kumarian Press, Inc.,
630 Oakwood Avenue, Suite 119, West Hartford, Connecticut 06110.

Cover design by Beth Gorman

Production supervised by Jenna Dixon
Text design by Jenna Dixon
Copyedited by Linda Lotz
Typeset by Sarah Albert
Proofread by Linda Faillace

Printed in the United States of America on recycled acid-free paper by
Thomson-Shore, Inc. Text printed with soy-based ink.

Library of Congress Cataloging-in-Publication Data

Henderson, Michael, 1932–
    All her paths are peace : women pioneers in peacemaking / Michael
Henderson.
        p.   cm. — (Kumarian Press books for a world that works)
    Includes bibliographical references.
    ISBN 1-56549-034-7 (pbk. : alk. paper). — ISBN 1-56549-035-5
(cl. : alk. paper)
    1. Women and peace—History. 2. Women pacifists—Biography.
I. Title. II. Title: Women pioneers in peacemaking. III. Series.
JX1962.A2H46   1994
327.1'72'082—dc20
                                     94-14748

---

98 97 96 95 94   5 4 3 2 1   1st Printing 1994

Dedicated to
Ellie Newton and Trudi Trüssel
who have pioneered in the spirit of Caux

CONTENTS

THE DALAI LAMA

ONE OF THE MAJOR challenges we continue to face at the close of the twentieth century is the achievement of genuine lasting world peace. In the past, the effects of war were limited, but today our potential for destruction is beyond imagination. In many parts of the world local and regional conflicts are causing misery to millions, and have potentially far-reaching global consequences.

Concerned groups and individuals everywhere have a responsibility to work for peace. We have an obligation to promote a new vision of society, one in which war has no place in resolving disputes among states, communities, or individuals, and in which nonviolence is the preeminent value in all human relations.

Many of the world's problems and conflicts arise because we have lost sight of the basic humanity that binds us all together as a human family. We tend to forget that despite the diversity of race, religion, ideology, and so forth, people are the same in their basic wishes for peace and happiness.

Michael Henderson has written a book that focuses on women as pioneers in creating peace. Women naturally have important roles to play in peacemaking. Nearly all of us receive our first lessons in peaceful living from our mothers because our need for love is the very foundation of human existence. From the earliest stages of our growth, we are completely dependent upon our mother's care and it is very important for us that she express her love. Since the very first thing we do is suck milk from our mother's breast, we naturally feel close to her. And she must feel love for us in order to feed us properly, otherwise her milk may not flow freely. Scientists suggest that if a child is not held, hugged, cuddled, or loved, its development will be impaired.

If children do not receive proper affection, in later life they will find it hard to love others. This is how a mother's love has a bearing on peace. Peaceful living is about trusting those on whom we depend and caring for those who depend on us. We receive our first experience of both those qualities in our relationship with our mother. I am not suggesting that motherhood be the only role for women, only that our mothers are powerful models for nearly all of us.

Everyone wishes to live in peace, but it is not achieved by merely talking or thinking about it, nor by waiting for someone else to do something about it. We each have to take responsibility as best we can within our own sphere of activity. I am sure that the examples set by women as mentioned in this book will inspire and encourage others. I pray that the contributions of women working for peace the world over may be blessed with success.

Dharmsala, May 27, 1994

ACKNOWLEDGMENTS

A BEAUTIFULLY PENNED twenty-four-page letter from eighty-one-year-old Yukika Sohma, one of a number of letters and faxes this Japanese pioneer sent to me, is an example of the generous cooperation I received from many women in putting together this book. Another is the care taken by Anna Marcondes in showing me around her *favela* in Rio and then, with the help of an interpreter, going through what I had written to be sure that it faithfully represented her struggle. So first, thanks must go to them and to Sushobha Barve, Audrey Burton, Antonia de Gallicchio, Heyde Durán, Agnes Hofmeyr, Shidzue Kato, Omnia Marzouk, Renee Pan, Berta Passweg, Edith Staton, and Abeba Tesfagiorgis, who were happy to open up their lives to me. It has been my good fortune to be well acquainted with almost all the women I wrote about, including the four who have died.

I would also like to thank the women from Creators of Peace for their cooperation and advice. Thanks, too, to Anne and Bryan Hamlin, Digna and Peter Hintzen, John Morrison, Evelyn and Luis Puig, and Randy Ruffin for their help with the creation of the book.

I am also grateful to Mary Lean and others from the staff of *For A Change* magazine, who had already written about some of the women. I appreciate the perspectives of Charis Waddy and owe thanks to a host of others in many countries who helped in different ways—including Kathy Aquilina, Satya Banerji, Hanni Blundell, Mike Brown, Dot and Dan Chapman, Paige Chargois, Catherine and Steve Dickinson, Karen Elliott, Aline Faunce, Yukihisa Fujita, Marcel Grandy, Peter Hannon, Joan Holland, Christine Jaulmes, Catherine Linton, Irene Massey, Kath Moir, 'Robo Orogun, Marlys Pierce, Jacqueline and Charles Piguet, Richard Ruffin, Marianne Spreng, Jigme Topgyal, Gordon Wise, and Denise and John Wood.

A special word of appreciation is due to Cynthia Sampson for her editing skills; to David Channer, who helped procure the photographs; to my wife, Erica, who read every word more than once; and to Kumarian Press, especially Krishna Sondhi, for keeping after me to produce a book. I am only sorry that space restrictions did not allow me to include many other women.

None of the above, of course, bears responsibility for the final product.

1

CREATORS OF PEACE

MARK TWAIN WAS ONCE ASKED, "In a world without women, what would men become?"

"Scarce, sir," replied Twain.

He could have added that men would be deprived of many of the influences that make life on earth more sensitive and caring.

One by one the ceilings, glass and otherwise, that have held women down are being shattered. Women's expectations of themselves and men's expectations of women are rising. One area that has not been explored adequately, however, is women's role in peacemaking. In some circles, the presence of women in combat is regarded as a great advance. Women in peacemaking would surely do more for the world.

For some years I have wanted to write a book about peace. As a journalist, I've made it a priority over the last forty years to encourage understanding among people of different backgrounds. I often felt that peace got a bad rap. During the cold war, the very word peace was discredited; it became politicized. Peace often became an excuse for blame, for an absence of thought, for an abundance of rhetoric. It was associated more with conflict than with harmony. My experience in many countries has convinced me that peace is more of a process than an objective. It is a fruit of new attitudes, a way of life that includes forgiveness and restitution.

I have met many men who have done great work for peace, including six winners of the Nobel Peace Prize. But as I look back, for some reason it is the women who stand out in my mind. First of all, my mother: She was Irish, and our family was forced to leave Ireland in 1922 for being Protestants, landowners, and, for several generations, police officers. My mother became a peacemaker when she went from being bitter about the way we were treated to facing up to the fact that Irish people felt as they did because of the way the English transplants had treated them.

I have met a number of women who are thinking along these same lines and have decided that they might be more effective in the world if they worked together. They call themselves Creators of Peace. One of the prime movers is an African woman, Anna Abdallah Msekwa, the Tanzanian minister of agriculture; another is the First Lady of Uganda, Janet Museveni. Anna Msekwa describes women as the missing link in the peacemaking chain and sees peacemaking in a broad dimension that includes the removal of poverty and hunger and the protection of the environment. Peace begins, she believes, in family life by "converting our homes into peace centers."

The women initiated a Creators of Peace conference at Caux, Switzerland (see page 171), in the summer of 1991 that was attended by 680 women and men from sixty-two countries. It was not a time for recrimination, said Mrs. Museveni, but a time of self-examination, "to find out where we have failed as women and as human beings and to resolve how we can begin to put right what went wrong."

Opening the conference, Swiss Senator Josi Meier said, "We women have to rewrite history. There can be no peace without the active collaboration of women. As mothers and potential mothers it is we who want life to go on." Madeleine Barot, an octogenarian from France who headed the department for women at the World Council of Churches and who has devoted most of her life to refugees, said, "Women are more sensitive to the injustices others are suffering, particularly strangers. This thirst for justice leads them to become peacemakers."

As I met with some of the women from Creators of Peace in 1993 and heard their plans for a follow-up conference, I thought that this would be the right moment for a book about women peacemakers. Obviously, there would be many candidates for such a book, so I decided to limit myself principally to women I knew and whose work I had observed firsthand over the years. I chose women of different continents, of different ages, of different political views, and of different faiths—Buddhist, Hindu, Jew, Muslim, and Christian, Protestant and Catholic. Five of the women— Japanese Senator Shidzue Kato, French Resistance fighter Irene Laure, Burmese educator Daw Nyein Tha, Irish trade unionist Saidie Patterson, and Papua New Guinea's first female Legislative Council member Alice Wedega—have written books or have had books written about them. The others are less well known. Their stories have never before been brought together. I chose them because their commitment illustrates the premise that peacemaking can be a way of life and because people would be able to identify with their experiences. I think it is fair to say that even the more high-profile women would deny that they had done anything out of the ordinary and would say, "You can do it too."

As we are confronted daily in the newspapers and on television with news of conflict and death, as bizarre women and men are given celebrity treatment and talk-show exposure, I encounter a widespread desire for better role models for young people. I believe that the women in this book are such models. I hope that their examples will inspire many others to pursue the paths of peace.

2

RECIPE FOR
RECONCILIATION

*A Hindu confronts prejudice against Muslims
and Sikhs in India.*

ANY COOK SHOULD BE ABLE to run the country,
according to Vladimir Lenin. But of course, he no longer has the
authority he once enjoyed. And to call Sushobha Barve a cook
hardly conveys the full dimension of this unconventional Indian
woman. There are those in India who believe that the kinds of
things she has done, at incredible personal risk, are what her country needs if it is to stay as one. And they began in the kitchen.

Trained in domestic science in Bombay, Sushobha, a high-caste
Hindu, went to work in 1969 in the kitchen at Asia Plateau. This
conference center in western India was set up by Rajmohan
Gandhi, a grandson of the Mahatma, as part of his commitment to
build a strong, clean, united India. Sushobha had been one of the
hundreds of young people who responded to his challenge to use
their lives to build a new country.

"The first two years were miserable," she remembers. "To begin
with, I didn't like cooking and I found it difficult to work behind
the scenes. Everyone else seemed to be doing much more interesting things. At home, cooking was something I didn't have to do."

But she persisted, deciding to accept responsibility for more than just cooking the meals. Along with other volunteers like her, she took to heart the concerns of the hundreds of people who came to the center. "Life became more interesting when I decided to be involved in helping the men and women from management and labor who came to the seminars on industrial relations instead of just thinking about the kitchen."

In 1979, Sushobha told a journalist that people in India needed to think on a larger scale, and not just about their own industries. She also said, "We need people who will dare to risk anything and everything to see things different."

In 1984, that is what she did. She was traveling in a train with a friend, Sarla Kapadia, when the news broke of Indian Prime Minister Indira Gandhi's murder by Sikhs. In their compartment were two Sikh businessmen.

At first there was an almost unnatural calm as the train journey continued. Fellow passengers discounted the Sikhs' fears of vengeance. But as the hours ticked by, the train began stopping, and there was a rumor that a Sikh had been pulled off the train and shaved—an affront to his faith. Sushobha and Sarla were concerned about protecting the Sikhs. Sushobha moved from the window to the door, and the men hid in the top bunk.

In one town, a gang of young people entered the compartment, but Sushobha managed to talk them out of causing trouble. At the next stop, however, the train was surrounded by villagers armed with sticks. Three times their compartment was searched. The fourth time the intruders wanted to know who was in the top bunk. They pulled off the sheet and discovered the two men. Sushobha tried to shield them and was seized. One man held her neck and hand. "How dare you assault a woman," she said. He let go and would not look her in the face. The Sikh men were pulled out, beaten until they seemed dead, and thrown back into the compartment; then everything was looted. When the train started again, it was discovered that the men were not dead. At the next stop, the two women could only watch helplessly as the bodies were thrown off, stoned, and set on fire. Sushobha and Sarla had been the only ones who tried to prevent the violence.

Thinking about the event shortly afterwards, Sushobha said that she never dreamt that her generation would witness killings comparable to those that took place after the partition of India and Pakistan in 1947, a period dramatized for the world through the film *Gandhi*. "It was gruesome," she wrote to a friend. "But even when the villager held me by the neck I felt comforted by God's love and protection. God gave me the right words to say which at least convinced one man. But," she asked, "what was God's purpose in allowing us to go through this? How are we going to repent and cleanse our sins? Is it possible to heal the wounds between Hindus and Sikhs?"

Sushobha had been brought up in an orthodox and broadminded Hindu family. Her parents and grandparents had always encouraged her to ask questions about religious beliefs and traditions and had inculcated a strong sense of right and wrong. "This did not prevent us from doing wrong, but we knew when we had strayed from the path, and our conscience would weigh heavily." She had never been taught to hate any religious, racial, linguistic or caste groups, but only rarely had people of different backgrounds intruded on the family's life. There had been little interaction with other religious communities.

An incident in college, however, had prepared her to be a bridge builder between the different religious communities in India. It was there that she had her first encounter with a Muslim—Abida, a fellow student with whom she shared a table. One day Abida spoke to Sushobha of her relatives who had come from Pakistan. This was only two years after India and Pakistan had been at war, and Sushobha suddenly found herself thinking that she could not trust Abida. Several months later, Sushobha had the uncomfortable thought that she should apologize to Abida for the invisible wall that she had allowed to grow between them. Her reaction to Abida brought into focus the unspoken prejudices and distrust that she feels are deeply embedded in the Hindu psyche. "How could I have allowed myself to be swayed emotionally and begun to distrust someone who had done no wrong to me?" she thought. "With this attitude there could be no hope of the various communities of India being able to live in harmony."

After Sushobha's apology, Abida was in tears. She had sensed that something had come between them, but she had not known what it was.

"This encounter opened the windows of my heart and set me off on a road to build friendship with Muslims right across the length and breadth of India," says Sushobha. "Since that day, distrust and prejudice toward Muslims have never brushed my mind or entered my heart. Somewhere along the line I realized that if true understanding was to come between people and communities I must also try to understand history from their viewpoint."

Sushobha describes the experience in the train as a watershed. "It not only shook me physically and emotionally but it made me realize that any one of us could become victims of violence in today's India." Many things that Sushobha had held precious had been shattered: her image of India as a secular nation; the vision that in spite of its shortcomings and difficulties, India's democracy would survive. Sushobha believed that national pride had been given a rude shock and that her country stood humiliated before the world. Yet she knew, too, that none of her emotions was going to help other people.

A month later, she was still feeling anger and guilt about those hours on the train. "I was tortured at night by the thought of not being able to save the lives of the two innocent men." She decided to accept the responsibility for what Hindus had done. There was a need for national repentance. The only way she could see this happening was by apologizing to the Sikhs unconditionally and asking for their forgiveness. "It was a painful process," she recalls, "but once accepted I was shown the steps I should take." She felt that she should write letters to Sikhs—some known by her, some not. As a Hindu, she wrote, she wanted to apologize unconditionally for what her people had done. She asked each one for forgiveness.

Khushwant Singh, a well-known writer and Sikh spokesman, replied in a handwritten note, "I was in tears as I read your letter. As long as we have people like you around we will survive as a nation."

It was one thing to write letters of that kind but another to visit Sikhs in person. Sushobha went to see a Sikh couple whose farmhouse had been attacked. Again she made an unconditional apology for the deep wounds and humiliation. Husband and wife were in tears. Usha, the wife, held her hand. "To hear what you have just said," she told Sushobha, "makes me feel that all we have gone through during the last two months was worth it and is healed."

But still Sushobha could not keep the image of the train victims out of her mind. She tried unsuccessfully to get information about them. Then came word that one of them might be alive. She had a compelling sense that she must travel the 1,200 miles to the place they came from. She would not have been open to it earlier, but she knew that she would have no peace of heart until she did so. She was fearful of how a Hindu would be received.

"I cannot express the joy I felt when I saw Bupendra Singh lying in his bed," she writes. "I was not greeted with hostility but with courtesy, not formally but as an old friend of the family." The room soon filled with family members, and as the story was pieced together, all felt that God had heard their prayers and not let them down. "It was a chain of miracles," believes Sushobha. She discovered that the other passenger, Govinder Singh, had also survived.

Bupendra recounted his story: As he lay on the ground pretending to be unconscious, he somehow managed to turn on his side and extinguish the fire. Govinder, who had been unconscious, was awakened by his skin burning. He too managed to get out of the burning clothes. In what seemed to be minutes, a group of police arrived and did their best to save them—this at a time when most police were inactive. The Sikhs remember that as they were carried, their bearers chanted *mantras* (prayers) for the dead. They were so badly burned that friends at the hospital did not recognize them. Besides body burns, Govinder needed 152 stitches in his head. The doctor asked the family, "Why have you brought me a dead body?" "It was a medical challenge," said Bupendra. "They struggled for two and a half hours to put life back into him, and he has just returned home."

Sushobha expressed her sorrow at not being able to protect them. "We feel bad that you had to suffer because of us," responded Bupendra. "We remember your arguing with those men and saw the first *lathi* [stick]. The men who took us talked of finding the women who were with us, and we were worried. We had not known what had become of you."

"Bupendra and his family were free of bitterness at a time when they had every reason to be bitter," says Sushobha. "Even the most inhuman suffering had not killed the fine human qualities of courage, compassion, vision of the future, and gratitude to all who had helped them—us, policemen, doctors, God for the gift of new life."

At a subsequent Dialogue on Development at Asia Plateau, Sushobha said, "Reconciliation and reconstruction of human lives and relationships is going to be a painful process. As we undertake this task at home, we will be shown how to build partnerships beyond our frontiers as well. The essential is men and women who are willing and dare to break the chain of hate and revenge."

From 1984 onward, after those traumatic hours in the train, Sushobha's work took on a new urgency. She consciously set out to build bridges of trust both within India and between India and her neighbors and to go where people were in particular need, sometimes taking teams of people with her. In 1988, for instance, Sushobha went with Tara Bhattarcharjee, a granddaughter of Mahatma Gandhi, and her daughter, Sukanya Bharatram, to Pakistan and Bangladesh. "Ordinary people need the chance to experience one another's warmth and hospitality," she says. "It is so much harder then to whip up feelings of hostility."

Earlier that year, Bangladesh had been in the news because of catastrophic floods and a cyclone that followed. "We wanted to be with the Bangladeshis in their time of tribulation," she says. They made a pilgrimage to the city of Noakhali, where Mahatma Gandhi had worked for three months in 1946 to make Noakhali a model for the subcontinent. At the time of his visit, there were widespread communal killings in Bengal and neighboring Bihar, and Gandhi's mission had been to replace fear and insecurity with courage, hatred with compassion, and blame with personal responsibility, and to discover with others a deeper understanding of the spirit of forgiveness and penance. It was, he said, one of the most difficult missions of his life. By the time he left, a relative peace had emerged. Shortly afterwards he was assassinated in Delhi.

In 1946, the Mahatma and his team had been greeted with hostility in Noakhali. This time, his granddaughter was welcomed with garlands, and her party was given a motorcycle escort to the Gandhi ashram. There they were greeted by eighty-eight-year-old Charu Chaudhury, one of Gandhi's original team. "It was a journey of redemption," says Sushobha. At the end of a prayer meeting, they went outside and walked, ankle deep in the mud, to the edge of a field, where Tara planted a mango tree in memory of the thousands who had died. Two young men washed the mud from Tara's feet with their hands. Tara was deeply moved by this act. "As I stood watching," Sushobha says, "I felt as if the past was cleansed and Gandhiji was blessing us from heaven."

In 1989, the Bhagalpur district in Bihar in eastern India was rocked by Hindu-Muslim clashes that took a thousand lives. Many people fled their homes and months later were still living in fear and in pitiful conditions. Sushobha, after going there to see for herself, appealed to people to come from all over India as an act of penance for what had been done to innocent people. There was a wholehearted response.

Sushobha and a team of twelve people took the time to listen to the villagers, who were numbed by sadness and anger and by an incomprehension of why this disaster had happened to them and were fearful of further attacks or revenge. The team members shared their own experiences of overcoming prejudice. At times, they were called on to mediate. They helped widows reconstruct their lives. The younger members of the team helped with the physical rebuilding. Sushobha describes how in one locality they were surrounded by seventy to eighty people and bombarded with questions: "The discussions that followed stressed the need to stop blaming someone else, to take responsibility for where each of us may have gone wrong and shed distrust and prejudice from our hearts. We saw the importance of leaving the past behind in order to build a new future." One man in the crowd remarked, "If we had held discussions like these before the riots, they would never have taken place."

Sushobha and her team were encouraged by women they met who refused to allow personal suffering to engender bitterness and blame against an entire community or group. "These men and women inspire us," she says, "in efforts to rebuild broken homes and lives on the debris and ashes of communal fires."

She describes how one evening they sat on the ground talking to a family whose home had been reduced to burnt and broken-down walls. They wondered why Indians had not learned from the trauma of the killings that had occurred after partition, why the communal carnage was being repeated. She said to the group, "Those who inflict such cruelty and destruction on others are neither Hindus nor Muslims. They are *Shaitans* [devils]. Those who are true believers of any religion would never commit such crimes." The old man of the family replied, "What you say is true. This is the work of devils. The reason is that we have lost our *Imaan* [faith]."

At the end of 1992, an event happened in India that threatened to destroy the very unity of the country, even its secular constitution. It was an event that showed Sushobha in her most courageous and wise light. It focused on the destruction of the Babri Mosque at Ayodhya, but its roots were deeply embedded in Indian history.

Nearly a thousand years before, a Muslim ruler had invaded India. Then, and subsequently, many Hindu shrines and temples were desecrated and destroyed, and in some cases, Muslim mosques were built on the sites. For years, militant Hindus had been demanding that these mosques be handed over. On December 6, thousands of Hindus converged on one of the most disputed of these sites, the five-hundred-year-old Babri Mosque, and tore it down with their bare hands. To Muslims, it devastated their faith in India, but to a large number of Hindus, including Sushobha, it was constitutionally and morally unacceptable. "It was an outrage," she says. She had expected something like that to happen, but even so, it was a shattering experience. She knew more clearly than many what would come afterwards.

In her own city of Bombay, the ten days of violence that followed left at least six hundred people dead and most of its nine million inhabitants fearful and in shock. Arson destroyed shops and business establishments belonging to Hindus and Muslims in most of the main market areas. As police remained passive, fear gripped rich and poor alike. Afraid of attacks from the "opposite" community, they barricaded themselves in their homes. According to opinion polls, India's Hindus were torn between remorse and justification.

Sushobha heard the news of the mosque's destruction at six o'clock in the evening and decided to meet with friends the next afternoon to see what could be done to forestall the bloodletting that she feared would follow. But by the next morning, the Bombay rioting had begun, and only a few could get through to the meeting. For the first forty-eight hours they could do little, though they felt an urgency to tell their Muslim friends that they understood their outrage and anguish.

Sushobha had an insistent thought that she should go to see the state governor and ask him to set up a citizens' peace committee so that at least some citizens who understood what was happening would have a chance to do something. She went with two others to the governor, who agreed with their suggestion and sent them on to the chief minister. That evening, the formation of the Citizens' Nonpolitical Peace Committee was announced. Sushobha was asked to serve on it.

Now equipped with a curfew pass, she was able to visit affected areas, grasp the scale of the problems, and recognize the need to concentrate relief efforts. A Hindu doctor she knew phoned her from another area, anxious because some Hindu boys had been beaten up and were now planning retaliation. Sushobha rushed across town to support her friend. She arrived in the middle of a meeting and was asked to speak. She told them that too much destruction had already taken place. Did they want to start another chain of rioting? Some of the young men challenged her to go tell the Muslims what she was telling them. She said that she would, but she did not know anyone in the Muslim areas. A woman offered to take her to a Muslim social worker.

The social worker, Amina Khan, asked Sushobha to come with her to the Hindu locality, where she apologized for what the young Muslims had done. Amina urged the Hindus not to retaliate and told them that she would intervene with the elders of her community to see that there was no more mischief. It was Amina who took Sushobha to the different localities in Dharavi, the largest

Sushobha Barve (second from right) in 1994 with Amina Khan (center), the social worker who took her to the Muslim parts of Dharavi, and residents of Dharavi. Photograph by Rahul Kapadia.

slum in Asia, home to some 750,000 people. There, at the beginning of January, a second wave of riots erupted.

One evening as Sushobha was trying to convince inhabitants of Dharavi not to flee and cause chaos at the railway stations, one woman said to her, "How dare you. You go away every evening. What right have you to tell us? You don't know what it means to be in a burning slum. You don't have to face the pelting stones and the fire." It shook her. She realized that she had no moral right to tell people to be fearless, to stay put and face the attackers, when she was not prepared to stay with them through the night. The next morning, much to the consternation of some members of the governor's Peace Committee, she said that she wanted to move into the area.

That afternoon, a serious situation was developing in a mosque area where a Muslim community felt trapped. Hundreds of young men were out in the streets. The atmosphere was frightening. A senior Muslim told Sushobha that he could not control the young men. He had told them to go and do what they liked. Sushobha said to him firmly, "I understand that you cannot control these young men, but I cannot accept that in my presence you will say to them to go out and do what they like. You have to take your words back." There was a stunned silence, because nobody ever spoke to him like that. Finally, he retracted his words. Sushobha then telephoned the police commissioner and suggested an army "white flag march" through the area. The white flags signified that they were on civil duty and would not open fire. He agreed and asked her to keep talking to the crowd until they came. Within half an hour the police, led by a Muslim additional commissioner, arrived and had a constructive meeting with the local citizens.

Sushobha was now sure that she should move into Dharavi. She did so, and for six nights she lived with a Muslim family right next to the mosque. It was a moving experience to find herself the only civilian walking the streets, getting valuable information about people who were sick and where food was running out, contacting doctors and bringing them to the area, treating policemen. Her handbag was full of cough mixture, aspirins, bandages, and other things for people. Meanwhile, she had her committee as a channel to the authorities.

While much of the rest of Bombay was burning in January, there was peace in Dharavi. Bombay citizens came out in the hundreds to help: company executives, doctors, nurses, academics, students. At one point, two hundred groups were involved in the relief work. The government, respecting them and realizing their effectiveness, was routing government relief through them.

By the end of January, sixty thousand people were in relief camps. The next challenge was to get them back to the areas from which they had fled; this required economic rehabilitation and the rebuilding of thousands of homes that had been destroyed. For instance, many of those involved in cottage industries in Dharavi, such as the garment and leather manufacturers, needed help in obtaining loans and work permits to get them back on their feet. Families of victims needed help getting compensation from the government. This sort of work was the priority of Sushobha and the relief groups when she spoke in Caux in 1993.

She was also involved in helping setting up peace meetings between communities and the citizen-police committees that would be attached to every police station. The goals of these committees were to defuse anger against the police for permitting destruction, to give both groups a sense of confidence, and to foster teamwork in maintaining harmony in the area. These committees were approved by the state government and the Bombay police commission. "We have great expectations for this," Sushobha told the *New York Times* (November 19, 1993). "Unless the people have a chance to meet face to face, they won't have a chance to talk. More rhetoric for communal harmony isn't enough. If we could make these citizens police committees work, in the long run they would help the social fabric of the city."

The healing process is a long one, she warns. Whenever there is a need, she is ready to stay in Dharavi where she is welcomed in the homes of families from the different communities.

For Sushobha, there were lessons to be learned from those weeks. If societies, communities, and democracy are not to disintegrate totally, citizens have to play their part actively and responsibly. As they demonstrate their readiness to take responsibility, a network of people can be formed at all levels: journalists, social workers, politicians, police.

"One day," she says, expressing another lesson, "I had the thought that I must pray for compassion also for the aggressor. For me, it meant praying for my own people with whose actions I had totally disagreed. It is important for those of us in crisis situations to keep our hearts open to listen to all sides. Unless we listen, we will never know how to help and we will never be used. When we listen, we are actually helping people toward finding solutions."

Sushobha believes that whatever the historical wrongs, the majority community has the greatest responsibility to maintain peace and harmony. "If the minorities feel insecure and afraid and suffer from a sense of grievance, the majority must reflect on what in their attitude has caused [the minorities] to have such feelings."

3

FOR THE LOVE OF
TOMORROW

*A French Resistance fighter builds bridges
across the Rhine.*

THE RAPID FRANCO-GERMAN reconciliation after
World War II is, according to Edward Luttwak, a leading military
strategist from the United States, "one of the greatest achievements
of modern statecraft." The experiences of one Frenchwoman, Irene
Laure, are a vivid example of what went into uniting two countries
that had fought three wars against each other in seventy years. The
desire that this former Resistance worker developed—in quite dramatic circumstances—to build bridges with the Germans was to
have far-reaching effects in Europe and an influence that continues
to this day in areas of ethnic conflict around the world. Klara
Agafonova, describing the work of Madame Laure in her Ukrai-
nian paper *Militseiski Kurier*, wrote on November 30, 1993: "Is
not our inability to rise above the hurts of our history the source of
the ethnic conflicts blazing in various parts of the former Soviet
Union? Trust and forgiveness. An open and sincere look into the
depths of one's soul. So simple, yet so difficult. But without it we
cannot survive."

The idea that she might meet Germans was not in Madame Laure's mind when she accepted an invitation to Caux in 1947. As one of the first female members of the French Parliament and as a member of the National Executive Council of the French Socialist party in charge of women's political action, she welcomed a visit to Switzerland. It would be a break from the pressures of political life and a chance for her and her children to enjoy some better food in a country that had been spared the wartime shortages they had endured. At that time, she believed that Germany would be best "wiped from the face of the earth."

Madame Laure's confrontation with Germans in Caux was different in nature but no less dramatic than a confrontation in her home city of Marseilles only three years earlier. It was the time of German occupation. Hunger was acute. For two months, a desperate population had been demanding an improvement in the distribution of food. Despite rationing, there was no meat, no butter, no potatoes. Two German officers had been killed by the Resistance movement, and the population's ration cards were going to be taken away in reprisal. Some knew who had done the killing, most did not, but no one was telling. It was a terrible time, with children dying of hunger.

Madame Laure decided to start a mass movement of women against the occupation policies that were causing the widespread hunger. She mounted a park bench in Aubagne, the suburb where she lived, and called for the women to come out the next day and show their support by joining her in a ten-mile march to the office of the *préfet*, the representative of the Vichy government, which was collaborating with Germany. She stipulated that it be a silent march and that the men stay home, as it would be too dangerous for them to demonstrate publicly. The next day, hundreds of women with their children assembled and started off toward the city, their numbers swelling as they went. When they reached the heart of the city where all the avenues converged, they were joined by women from other parts until they numbered in the thousands.

The gates to the prefecture, the city offices, were shut, but Madame Laure and a few other women were permitted to slip through. They went up the ornate stairs and into the *préfet*'s office and approached the oak table behind which he sat. To the side of the room stood the German authorities.

"You are embarked on a dangerous course," the *préfet* told the women. "You run the risk of being put in prison."

"Yes, I know," said Madame Laure, "but if anything happens to me, I wouldn't give much for your skin."

The *préfet*, she remembers, went pale. He knew that it was no empty threat. He could see the silent crowd in the square below. "I cannot do anything," he said, "speak to the Germans there." The Germans, who understood French, had taken in the exchange. They said that they would consider her demands and told her to leave.

Coming out into the square, the women found it ringed with men with machine guns trained on their legs. Madame Laure was quickly shielded by the women and spirited into an unguarded side lane, down which she escaped. She boarded a tram back to her suburb. All along the route, French and German police were looking for her. Through her nursing work and her Resistance activities she was known to most people, but nobody gave her away. On arrival at her tram stop, she was met by the local chief of police. Something he said made her realize that he too was in the Resistance. She was safe.

Early in life, Madame Laure developed the steel to resist wrongs and a social conscience that would not rest. She was born in 1898 in Switzerland to a Swiss mother and had her early schooling there. Her Italian father had a construction company and was helping to build the first cable railway from Chamonix to Les Bossons. Observing how poorly he treated his workers, she stole chocolate and sugar and even his socks for them, putting herself at odds with him. "It was when my feelings for the workers of the world came alive," she told one interviewer. As a teenager, she heard of a group of people who believed that exploitation could be ended. "When you're sixteen, you're curious and go to see for yourself. I was fascinated." That was the beginning of a lifelong identification with the Socialist party.

During World War I, she worked as a nurse in the south of

France, attending to thousands of badly wounded soldiers. The authorities brought them in by train at night so that the general population would not be unnerved. After the war she married Victor, a sailor and, like herself, a Marxist with no faith in God. They had five children and raised nine others as well. When the Socialist party split in two, she joined Léon Blum's wing; her husband, though inclined to go with the Communists, followed her. Later he would admit that it was the right choice. In those interwar years, they tried as Socialists to build bridges between countries and friendships with the Germans, even taking German children into their home and working to save children caught up in the Spanish civil war.

When France was taken over by the Germans in World War II, the Laure family threw in their lot with the Resistance. Madame Laure's son was tortured by the Gestapo. When Allied bombers flew overhead, she rejoiced at the destruction that would be wreaked on Germany. After the war she witnessed the opening of a mass grave containing the mutilated bodies of some of her comrades. She longed for the total destruction of Germany; she never thought that understanding was possible, never sought it.

In 1946 she was elected to Parliament in Paris with a huge majority. It was the first time women had been able to vote or stand for Parliament, and thirty-three of them were elected. But even on social policies affecting women, they would not cross party lines. Madame Laure became more and more frustrated and was tempted to retire to the local scene, to go back to nursing.

It was at that point that she received the invitation to Caux. She was skeptical, thinking that it might be a capitalist trap, but as a Socialist she felt that she should at least investigate any idea that might be of assistance. She went in 1947 with her two youngest children, Claude and Juliette, whose bodies had suffered badly from malnutrition. She found the setting magnificent, but to her horror, 150 Germans arrived while she was there, the first large group to be permitted to leave the country after the war. No matter that many of them were victims of Hitler, had suffered in concentration camps, or had fought the regime. To her, they were Germans.

When one of them spoke from the platform, she got up and walked out. "It was a physical reaction," she recalled.

She was determined to leave the conference but hesitated when challenged with the question of how Europe could ever be rebuilt without including the Germans. Her immediate response was that anyone who made such a suggestion had no idea what she had lived through. Her internationalism had been diminished by her war-time experiences. Her second response was that perhaps there might be hope of doing something differently, though she still needed the spiritual experience that could break the steel band of hatred for Germans that encased her heart.

She shut herself in her room, wrestling with the question of whether she would be willing to give up that hatred for the sake of a new Europe. "I was there two days and nights without sleeping or eating with this terrible battle going on inside me. I had to face the fact that hatred, whatever the reasons for it, is always a factor that creates new wars." At Caux she had heard the idea that if you were 10 percent in the wrong it was your business to put it right, even if 90 percent of the wrong was not yours. "But I was not only 10 percent wrong, I was 90 percent wrong," she said.

On the third morning, Madame Laure was ready to have a meal with a German woman. She hardly touched her food but poured out all she felt and all she had lived through. And then she said, "I'm telling you all this because I want to be free of this hate." There was a silence and then the German woman, Clarita von Trott, shared with the French woman her experiences from the war. Her husband, Adam, had been one of those at the heart of the July 20, 1944, plot to kill Hitler. It had failed and he had been executed, and she was left alone to bring up their two children. She told Madame Laure, "We Germans did not resist enough, we did not resist early enough and on a scale that was big enough, and we brought on you and ourselves and the world endless agony and suffering. I want to say I am sorry."

After the meal, the two women and their interpreters sat quietly on the terrace overlooking Lake Geneva. Then Madame Laure, the Marxist Socialist, told her new German friend that she believed that if they prayed, God would help them. She prayed first, asking to be freed of hatred so that a new future could be built. And then Frau von Trott prayed, in French. Instinctively, Irene laid her hand on the knee of her former enemy. "In that moment," she said later, "the bridge across the Rhine was built and that bridge always held, never broke."

Madame Laure asked to be given the opportunity to speak to the conference. Many knew her background, but few knew what conclusion she had come to alone in her room or the effect that her conversation with Frau von Trott had had on her attitude. "Everyone was fearful. They knew what I felt about the Germans. They didn't know I had accepted the challenge."

Speaking to the six hundred people in the hall, including the Germans, she told them honestly and, as she says, disastrously, all that she had felt. But then she went on, "I have so hated Germany that I wanted to see her erased from the map of Europe. But I have seen here that my hatred is wrong. I am sorry and I wish to ask the forgiveness of all the Germans present. One cannot forget, but one can forgive." Following her words a German woman stepped up from the hall and took her hand. To Irene it was such a feeling of liberation that it was like a great weight being lifted from her shoulders. "At that moment I knew, I literally knew, that I was going to give the rest of my life to take this message of forgiveness and reconciliation to the world."

British historian Robin Mowat, in his book, *Decline and Renewal*, describes the effect of Madame Laure's apology on the Germans as "electric." He writes, "One of them related that he could not sleep for several nights—his 'whole past was in revolt at the courage of this woman'" (p. 197).

Peter Petersen, later to become a member of the German parliament, had been ready to answer back if Madame Laure attacked the Germans. But, as he said later, it was so different from what he had expected. "I was dumbfounded. We knew, my friends and I, that she had shown us the only way open to Germany if we wanted to join in the reconstruction of Europe."

Rosemarie Haver, whose mother was the woman who took Madame Laure's outstretched hand, said to her in Caux in 1984,

"Your courage in bringing your hatred to God and asking us Germans for forgiveness was a deeply shattering experience. When I saw my mother go up to you, my whole world collapsed about me. I felt deeply ashamed at what Germans had done to you and your family. I slowly began to understand that these Germans who had also brought much suffering on my own family had acted in the name of Germany, which meant in my name also."

Madame Laure and her husband decided to go to Germany. For eleven weeks they crisscrossed the country addressing two hundred meetings, including ten of the eleven state parliaments. With them went some of their compatriots who had lost families in the gas chambers, as well as men and women from other countries who only a short time before had been fighting against the Germans. All of them had found a willingness to forgive the past.

They spoke to trade unions and to "Ruhr barons." "The day that I was in the home of the Krupp family and I spoke to the mother of the family, I sensed deeply in my heart what went through the hearts of mothers when war was in the world," said Madame Laure. "She was a woman formerly of immense wealth who had lost everything."

The Laures went to Berlin on the airlift. "When you have seen with your own eyes the ruins of Berlin, you have a suffering in your heart that vows that those things shall never happen again." In fact, she told a group of women clearing away rubble, "I swear to you that I will give the rest of my life so that what you are going through will never again be possible in the world."

It was not always easy. At one point, as she was driving, she caught sight of a signpost for Dachau and suddenly felt that she was going out of her mind. Was she betraying those who had died? Then came a reassuring voice from within: "You're on the right path."

Journalist David Price, in a master's dissertation at Queen Mary College, London, wrote, "Irene Laure and many others like her undoubtedly affected thousands in their speeches throughout Germany. Adenauer is quoted as saying, in 1958, that Victor and Irene Laure had done more in the past 15 years than any other two people to build unity between the age-old enemies, France and Germany."

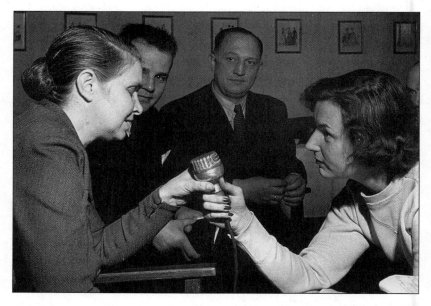

Irene Laure apologizes to the Germans over Berlin radio in 1949. Photograph by Peter Sisam.

The new approach Madame Laure had found to the Germans affected her attitude toward everyone. In her family, for instance, her daughter noticed that she no longer nagged. The Laures refound the faith in which they had been brought up and were remarried in church, in the presence of five children, two sons-in-law, and four grandchildren. "It isn't every day that a son of twenty-five witnesses the real marriage of his parents," said son Louis. Later, a granddaughter married a German, and Madame Laure fully supported her.

Le silence, quiet time, became a valued part of her family's life. She wrote down her thoughts in a notebook. She saw this practice in a broad dimension. "Instead of dropping bombs or firing guns, be quiet and listen. For some it is the voice of God, for others the voice of conscience; but every one of us, man or woman, has the chance to take part in a new world, if we know how to listen in quiet to what is in our hearts."

She began to move beyond class war in her thinking about

employers. She saw that they too could play a part in putting right what was wrong in the world. This had an effect on industrial relations in the north of France, particularly through a bridge she built with the representative of the employers, Robert Tilge. Together they organized an industrial conference in Le Touquet, which, according to the regional paper *Voix du Nord,* created "a state of mind favorable to the discovery and application of solutions." Her humility and her freedom from bitterness also played a part in Tunisia's move toward independence from France without the bloodshed that plagued Algeria. As she said after a visit to Tunisia, "If one wants freedom for oneself, one must be ready to give it to others. It is the only way to preserve one's own freedom."

She began to see a positive role for the United States which she had previously felt only wanted to exploit her country. This change of heart happened in 1947 as she watched General Marshall, whom she had mistrusted in the past, outline his plan to send aid to Europe before the U.S. Senate Foreign Relations Committee. In later years she would visit the United States nine times and apologize to Americans for Europe's failure to solve its own problems, which had led to the sacrifice of American lives.

At Caux she welcomed the industrial delegations from France, the nationalist leaders of North Africa, even her own Foreign Minister Robert Schuman, who told a conference session, "I am accustomed to international conferences. They usually end with great disappointments. Here we find nothing but satisfaction and a great hope. I will never give up."

She traveled all over the world to carry her answer of forgiveness. After speaking to four hundred children in Japan, she was asked by a twelve-year-old, "Are you for or against the French revolution?" She replied, "I am for revolution. But I have discovered that instead of liquidating the people you are against, you can change them, which is much more effective."

On one of nine trips to India, she was asked by an Indian businessman for the secret of her youthfulness. She responded, "Being convinced about what you undertake and giving yourself to it without reservation."

After she had related her convictions to Golda Meir, the Israeli prime minister said, "How encouraging it is to meet someone who hasn't given up the fight. Thank you for coming to see me. It is a great honor."

She met the Sami people in Sweden, the Maoris of New Zealand, the Aborigines of Australia, the native Americans. She challenged them to be a bridge between the Third World and the affluent world.

"It took a miracle to uproot the hatred in my heart. I barely believed in God, but he performed this miracle. I became free to struggle for the whole world, with a deep desire to heal the past. After I asked the Germans for forgiveness for having wished their country's complete destruction, I was finally able to work effectively for world peace."

Irene Laure died in La Ciotat, near Marseilles, in 1987 at the age of eighty-eight. An obituary in the *London Times* (July 16, 1987) was headlined, "Resistance heroine and healer of wounds." It described how "she went to work tirelessly to reconcile France and Germany."

Her influence lives on, in part through a biography, *For the Love of Tomorrow*, which has been published in French, German, and English. Its author, Swiss writer Jacqueline Piguet, sums up the Frenchwoman as "committed to help those who suffer, living a Socialism of heart and generosity but never bound by doctrinal or political points of view, with the turning point in her life the discovery of the power of forgiveness." A film of her life with the same title has been dubbed into eighteen languages. The French Foreign Ministry gave a grant in 1993 for the dubbing of the video into the Khmer language for Cambodia, where it is being used by human rights organizations in their educational training programs. Renee Pan (see Chapter 4), one of those behind the decision to dub the film into Khmer, does not see a Frenchwoman in the film, she says, but a Cambodian woman.

Madame Laure lives on, too, in the lives of other men and women who, like Renee Pan, say that they have been inspired by her example to take action in their own countries on the same basis. Eliezer Cifuentes, a Guatemalan who was attacked by gunmen for his reform work, remembers the first time he watched the film about Madame Laure: "I saw the tigers of hatred in my heart for the military and for the United States which I felt was backing them. I found a renewal inside that began to change my feelings of hatred and my desire for revenge." He began to apply what Madame Laure had done between the French and Germans to the conflicting elements in his society.

On yet another continent, Abeba Tesfagiorgis (see Chapter 5), in an Eritrean prison, found through Madame Laure's example the courage to see beyond the threats of her torturers. "Just as Irene Laure could not hope to see a united and peaceful Europe without Germany," she told her fellow prisoners, "we could not say we love our country and then refuse to understand and forgive our fellow Eritreans."

Joseph Montville, a former U.S. diplomat skilled in nonofficial diplomacy, sees the experience of Madame Laure as a model for relieving that sense of victimhood, and the violence associated with it, that usually defies traditional solutions. Although it is rare for national leaders to admit past national misdeeds, he believes that individual representatives like Laure can assume such responsibility. By their acts of forgiveness or contrition, they then become spokespersons for a new way of thinking and a new image for their respective nations. "The actual initiatives in accepting responsibility and asking forgiveness," he writes, "were not necessarily taken by high-level leaders, but rather by persons who had or came to have the confidence and respect of their leaders."

Hal Saunders, a former U.S. assistant secretary of state, said in 1992, "If the changes in the human arena involving the French and German people who came to Caux after 1945, if that human relationship had not been changed, there would be no institutions of the European community today, or they would at least have taken longer in coming."

4

FREEING UP SOME MEGABYTES

*A surprising legacy of the killing fields—a
Cambodian computer expert taps into a
new creativity.*

"HONEY, YOU MUST LEAVE. I must stay. I'll see you
again when Cambodia is at peace." Those were among the last
words Renee Pan heard from her husband, Sothi, deputy prime
minister of Cambodia, just five days before Pol Pot's Khmer Rouge
took over Phnom Penh on April 17, 1975. "I was waiting for him
at the U.S. embassy when this message came." Only an hour or so
earlier had come an urgent phone call from the U.S. ambassador to
inform the family that the Americans were leaving and to invite the
Pan family to come with them. On the way to the embassy, Sothi
decided to stop at the prime minister's office to inform him and to
join a meeting of the government ministers. He asked Renee to
send the car back for him, but he never arrived at the airport. As
she was whisked away to safety in a helicopter, she was in a confused state. "My only thought was that I would take care of the
children and he would take care of the country," she said. She does
not know what prevented him from coming; she stayed in Bangkok
for a month, waiting for him in vain. But as much as she wanted

him to come, she is sure that it was his love of his country that kept him there.

Peace has come to Cambodia, but sadly, Renee must assume that Sothi is dead. When last heard of, he was a prisoner of the Khmer Rouge. Like every other Cambodian, she carries the sorrow of family losses; in two decades of violence, an estimated three million people, or half the population, lost their lives. Renee believes that Sothi would have been proud of the way she brought up their three children single-handedly, founded the Cambodian Children's Education Fund, and is now working to help Cambodia develop its democratic infrastructure. While she lived in exile in the United States through the 1980s, Renee never dreamed that her country would experience such a sudden and dramatic turnaround and that two decisions she made there—to learn computing and to give up her hatred of the Khmer Rouge—would prove so valuable to the new country.

Renee was born to a part-Cambodian, part-French father and a Vietnamese mother. Growing up she took this fact for granted, but later she came to resent the confusion of three nationalities, since both the French and the Vietnamese had hurt her country. "I wanted to be a Cambodian," she said. She was raised as a Buddhist. The family was poor, and when Renee was in junior high school, she was adopted by a wealthy aunt who had no children.

In high school she fell in love with Sothi, who had been tutoring her. It was seven years before they married, and then only when she extracted a promise from him that she could go back to school. In 1960, when they married, her husband had just received a B.S. from Ohio University in mining engineering and was teaching math at a technical school. A year later, after their first son, Noren, was born, her husband received a scholarship for further education in the United States. She joined him there a year later, after she had gained her baccalaureate. In the United States, she earned a B.S. in mathematics while Sothi got a Ph.D. in education, statistics, and psychology. They also had their second child, Ravin. Dan Chapman, a fellow student of Sothi's, remembers Renee's excellent cooking, including such delicacies as alligator eggs and spring rolls. The Chapmans and the Pans helped each other understand their respective cultures. Dan's wife, Dot, typed Renee's dissertation. The Pans then moved to New Philadelphia, Ohio, where Sothi was a consultant at the board of education and Renee taught at the high school. There, Dan says, the Pans came up against racial prejudice. They kept a collection of stuffed animals in the window of their rented house, and some people concluded that the animals were displayed for religious purposes. They started a campaign to make the Pans feel unwelcome. When a roach infestation was reported at the Pans' house, considerable damage was done while "investigating." The landlord made the Pans pay for the damages. By pooling their resources, the Pans and Chapmans were able to buy a house and move in together.

Two years later, in 1969, the Pans returned to Cambodia, despite a dangerous political situation. Their third child, Sothira, was born in Phnom Penh. Renee's husband worked at the mines and taught at university. Then, the following year, Prince Sihanouk was deposed and a new government was formed. Sothi, who had been interested in politics since his student days, when he wanted to liberate his country from the French, was appointed the government's roving ambassador to the African countries and sub-sequently minister of education. He became general secretary of the Republican party, whose president was Lon Nol. In 1973, he was elected vice president of the National Assembly, and in 1974, he was appointed deputy prime minister. Meanwhile, Renee taught in the one English-language high school and then became director of the Ministry of Culture, where she was able to implement inte-grated science and introduce modern math.

After the Khmer Rouge takeover, her dramatic flight out, and the wait in Bangkok, Renee went to the United States. Their old friends the Chapmans were supportive, and thanks to a scholarship and help from the university, the Lutheran church, and the gov-ernment, Renee was able to continue her studies at the University of North Dakota, where she got her master's degree in statistics and computer science. She was then transferred by the company she worked for to St. Paul, Minnesota, where she became an eco-nomic forecaster for a pool of power companies.

As a refugee, she struggled first to become economically

independent. It took her four years to do so, and then she decided to devote her time, money, and energy to the welfare of her community and country. She was encouraged in this goal by remembering what her parents had told her as she grew up: Good deeds receive good deeds, they would say; and, quoting Buddha, a good deed will follow you like your own shadow, while bad deeds are like the trace left behind by the wheel of an oxcart.

As well as helping Southeast Asian refugees settle and serving on the Minnesota State Advisory Council on Refugees, she became politically involved in the Khmer People's National Liberation Front (KPNLF), which was trying to help Cambodia free itself from Vietnamese occupation. Renee, however, soon became discouraged by the divisions within the KPNLF which undermined its effectiveness. She wrote to many of the key leaders to express her discontent and to put the blame on them. She had hoped to clear up the situation, but this action seemed only to create more mistrust among the free Cambodians.

She had reached a point in her life, she says, where she did not have anything to give. "My energy did not regenerate itself," she recalls, "my brain was empty and my heart was numb and insensitive. I got angry very easily, hated bad people, was unhappy, selfish, and did things foolishly." She wondered if she should quit.

It was during this time, in 1985, that she saw *For the Love of Tomorrow*, the film about Irene Laure. The fact that Irene—a Frenchwoman whose son had been tortured by the Germans— would be willing to forgive them made Renee think that perhaps this was the key to dealing with the Khmer Rouge. Hearing that she could meet Madame Laure in Caux, Renee accepted an invitation to go there that summer.

At Caux, she was struck by the fact that there were no walls between people of different backgrounds; she felt that all the people there were her friends. She did everything she could to help, including serving in the dining room and cooking. She enjoyed the session called "From Conflict to Cure," but was she ready to take the necessary steps in her own life? "Every night I had a fight with myself," she recalls. She met Irene Laure and immediately asked her what the key was to this new approach, how had she been able to accomplish what she did? "How do you find forgiveness?" Irene said very simply that the key was to have quiet time alone. The ten-minute talk with the Frenchwoman had a profound effect on Renee.

Like Irene, Renee spoke from the platform. Out of her experiments with quiet time and meditation had come the idea to forgive the Khmer Rouge and to ask them to forgive her for her thoughts. This she declared publicly. But, as she said later, it was one thing to do that among friends in Caux and another to do it face-to-face with the Khmer Rouge. "It was very hard for me to forgive the Khmer Rouge for what they did to me, to my family and my friends, and especially to my beloved country," she says, "but the burden of revenge that I carried for a decade was lightened from the moment that I did so." She said at the time, before it became clear that some kind of reconciliation would be indispensable for a political solution, "I am sometimes accused by other Cambodian friends of supporting the Khmer Rouge because I refuse to accuse them, but if I kill the Khmer Rouge, I will become like one of them."

Renee realized that her mind had been consumed by what her Buddhist religion calls the "three fires of the world"—greed, anger, and foolishness. She decided that from then on she would have a time of quiet each day to provide, as she calls it, "an indispensable food to nurture my mind." Through these quiet times, the teachings of Buddha became real to her for the first time. "It became less hard," she says, "to endure the discipline that leads to enlightenment."

She started to ask her friends to forgive her "for putting them down on many occasions, despising them, getting angry and cutting conversations with them." She thought about her abortive attempts to bring unity among the Cambodians. She decided to meet with the KPNLF president and apologize to him. Before she left home that morning, she asked Buddha for the courage to do so. "I was ready," she says, "to accept the consequences without fear of losing face or friends." As well as making a verbal apology, she wrote a letter that was made public. "Finally, the pardon was given," she says. "I felt such relief." And far from losing friends as she had feared, she was admired for her action. Later she would find that her attitude of blame and hatred toward King Sihanouk and his queen could also be turned into love and compassion.

The periods of quiet reflection and the change in attitude toward other people affected her relations with her family. "In our tradition it is not easy for an adult to ask forgiveness from a younger person," she says. "It took me quite a while to do it, especially with my own children."

As a computer specialist, Renee likes to use computer images to describe what has happened to her. Human memory, she maintains, is unlimited compared with computer memory, but if the memory is loaded with impurities, it is unable to solve even a simple problem. "Forgiveness freed up some megabytes in my memory," she told a conference in Atlanta in 1987. "I dare to solve problems on a larger scale, with less CPU [central processing unit] time, in a more efficient way."

Another result of this change in her life was her decision to become less involved in politics and more involved in the future education of her people. In 1988, she founded in Minnesota the Cambodian Children's Education Fund [CCEF], with the aim of developing "education for all." At that time, its operations were confined to the refugee camps on the Thai-Cambodian border, since it was not possible to function within Cambodia. "The purpose was to finish the unfinished work left by my husband and to heal the wounds"—and to do what also was almost unheard of: to work with all factions.

Aiming to enhance the work of existing organizations, CCEF sent out task forces to talk with Cambodian educators in the camps and identify gaps in educational programs. The Thai Ministry of Education invited CCEF to develop a program on education for Cambodian repatriation. Twelve-week courses were instituted at Buriram Teachers' College. Curriculum development was a cooperative project with the Cambodian educators, Buriram, and CCEF working together. The students came from the camps of the different political factions. Renee fearlessly accompanied Khmer Rouge officers alone to their camp. "I delivered a powerful speech in front of forty Khmer Rouge teachers, powerful because I talked to the real Khmer Rouge, while at Caux it was to friends. I was quiet and calm. I knew that the hatred was over at that moment. The hatred came and left freely within me and I had no way to control it." Afterwards the officers drove her home. One of them asked, "Can the world ever forgive us?"

With the prospect of democratic rule returning to Cambodia, plans were laid to launch CCEF in the country. But what was most gratifying to Renee was that by the end of 1993, many of the more than fifty graduates of the first courses were employed in leadership positions in the country. She is aware that a recent World Bank study showed that industrial growth in high-performing Asian nations is closely linked to the priority put on education. The current goals of CCEF are to understand the role of education in a free society, to recognize and support the cultural heritage of the Khmer, and to introduce strategies of dialogue, critical thinking, and problem solving. Although based in Minnesota, CCEF is sensitive to Cambodian culture and recognizes that Western values must not be imposed. In a culture that has traditionally educated only a select few and has systematically excluded women, however, its approach represents a substantial departure.

With the dramatic changes brought about by the Paris Agreement of October 23, 1991, Renee was able to return to her country—first to investigate the possibility of launching CCEF there, and then, motivated by the feeling that her place was with her people, to assist in the return to democracy. She accepted an invitation to work with the United Nations Transitional Authority in Cambodia [UNTAC], which was overseeing the transition of authority from a one-party communist state to a multiparty democracy under a constitutional monarch. World opinion did not hold out much hope for the success of the UN operation or the readiness of the Cambodian people to come together after decades of civil war. There was little experience on which to build and years of communist indoctrination to overcome.

For nearly two years, Renee worked with the UN as it conducted its largest, most ambitious, and most expensive peacekeeping operation ever. At its peak, it involved 22,000 military, police, and civilian personnel, at a cost to the world community of $2 billion.

Renee Pan (right) meets an old friend in Phnom Penh in 1992 for the first time since the Khmer Rouge takeover. Photograph by David Channer.

Her work was as a translator and then as a radio producer, and she traveled all over the country by road and by helicopter. She had to translate anything that had to do with the elections, including ballot papers, regulations, and posters. "It was a chance to use the language ordinary people understood," she says. She also had to translate all kinds of laws—property laws, land law—and manuals for the different departments, such as immigration, and for the foreign affairs and finance ministries. She went out with UNTAC specialists to the provinces to train tax collectors, the public, and the police and took part in dangerous investigations of crimes and illegal transactions—on one occasion sitting down with a murderer. "I realized that my translating job was essential to the creation of a safe environment for the election," she says.

Her work tied in with her new convictions about individual responsibility. In October 1992 she wrote to a friend: "I am in a team of five Cambodians translating documents. Honesty is my main preoccupation. There is a lot of stealing in each office. We have to learn to be honest in order to help rebuild our nation. Honesty gives a better life to you all and it is a tool to cut the root of corruption."

During this run-up to the election, much of her energy went into voluntary work with a network of friends to help prepare the country. She held planning meetings in her home, where they came up with imaginative ideas for seminars and roundtables to bring conflicting factions together to discuss issues such as human rights and the moral basis for a free democracy.

In February 1993, she interrupted her work to make a memorable trip to Vietnam to visit her parents, from whom she had been estranged. She had seldom written to them over the years, and she realized that her attitude toward them had been wrong. "The trip back home was excellent. Every day was a blessing. Everything happened like a miracle." Renee's sister introduced her to her mother as a friend, but she was soon recognized, and there were "a lot of tears as we hugged each other the whole day." Renee called it a breakthrough. "We reconciled all the bad feelings, and the feeling of not belonging was gone. I was able to conduct conflict resolution within my family. Each one had harbored bad feelings about the others for so many years and had never dared to talk face to face. They asked forgiveness from each other. It was fun. I was even able to help my father to realize his dream of having a brick house for his family."

Renee wants to use all her experiences to help the people of Vietnam someday. She says that the trip back home reminded her of her visit to Sri Lanka five years earlier. "The statue of the Lord Buddha from that holy place in Kandy sits in my living room and provides me with everything. I adore him and pray every day in front of him to express my gratitude. The Lord Buddha taught me to liberate myself from all attachments and ill will. My fear, my grief never surfaced while I was in Phnom Penh. At Kandy I made two wishes: one, to know how my husband died; two, to be able to implement the educational project in Cambodia. One of them already came about, and the other is in the process of emerging."

Immediately before the election in March 1993, she and some

friends held a two-day international seminar entitled "Confidence Building for Peace in Cambodia." It was attended by political leaders, UN volunteers, university students, foreign diplomats, and members of the Buddhist hierarchy, including the international patriarch, venerable Maha Ghosananda, who gave the invocation. "To make peace," he said, "the skills of teamwork and cooperation are essential. There is little we can do for peace as long as we feel we are the only ones who know the way to build it." That seminar led to the creation of a Committee for National Reconciliation. Before the election, Ghosananda also led *Dharma yatra*, a peace march from the Thai-Cambodian border to Phnom Penh, and Renee took one day to participate in that.

Renee and her friends produced and had printed thousands of copies of a handbook on democracy, *Which Way, Cambodia?*, in English and Khmer. It quotes the Buddha: "Hatred does not cease by hatred. Easily seen are the faults of others but one's own faults are hard to see . . . conquer the angry man by love; conquer the miser with generosity; conquer the liar with truth." Meanwhile, several hundred copies of a Khmer version of the video about Irene Laure's life, *For the Love of Tomorrow*, were distributed around the country and shown on national television.

As well as continuing her translation work, Renee helped the UN radio develop strategies that could reduce intimidation and fear. In fact, UNTAC radio and the information it supplied played a significant role in convincing people that they could vote secretly and freely. "Classical Cambodian music was aired often," she says, "to calm down the greed and the violence, and to make Cambodians think more of their rich culture and to set aside their differences." During the May 23–28 elections Renee worked as one of the international polling station supervisors. Ten thousand UN troops armed with rifles and wearing flak jackets were deployed at fifteen hundred polling stations to cope with the predicted violence and intimidation.

"Shock in Cambodia—nobody killed," proclaimed a headline in the London *Economist* at the end of the month. The magazine noted that, instead of a body count, the UN-supervised elections were marked by a high vote count—85 percent of registered voters. Despite threats from the Khmer Rouge, the Cambodian elections had gone off peacefully. One UN monitor reported that police had to be employed not to stop violence but to restrain overeager voters as they poured into the polling station. The Australian ambassador said that in one village, police, seeing crowds moving in distant hills, feared a Khmer Rouge attack. The movement turned out to be whole families, dressed in their temple best and led by older women, coming to vote. The UN representative in Cambodia, Yasushi Akashi, said, "We were sustained by the great courage of the Cambodian people, and this is what saved the situation. Despite all the difficulties, obstacles, and even threats to their lives, they went to vote."

Renee continued as a radio producer for three months after the election. Her program was broadcast four times a week under the title, "Vision for Cambodia Year 2000." The format was a roundtable discussion about culture, education, sciences, technology, and health.

According to Renee, the UNTAC operation will be remembered as "the Cambodian renaissance period." She is grateful for the way the world community rallied to support her country. It was an exciting time for her. "I got the chance to fully use my knowledge, fully exercise my compassion, fully express my gratitude to my beloved country, fully use my quiet time."

During the transition, the electronic data processing (EDP) unit was looking for Cambodians to take charge of the military payroll—a complicated affair, with the four political factions having to learn to work together. They enlisted Renee. From the military payroll, she moved on to the payrolls of the police and the civil service. The computer proved to be too small for the job, and the appropriate computer and program were requested from and supplied by UNTAC. "The payroll gave rise to a safe future for Cambodia," says Renee. "It is the starting point for development, since the diversity of systems in the country was the source of a lot of the problems. I have the opportunity to standardize the system, unite the diversity. My scientific knowledge and my acquaintance with the Western system was put to maximum use. The whole business of me getting involved with the computer system was not in my thoughts before I left the United States. Only God knew it."

On September 21, 1993, a new constitution was adopted that expressed a commitment to liberal democracy, the rule of law, and women's rights. Implementation is now one of Renee's concerns. "Human rights come to town. People talk about it, write it in the constitution, millions of dollars are spent, but the impact is insignificant, especially to women's and children's rights," she says. "I am patient in most areas, but I cannot hold out anymore in this situation."

She is helping women who work in government—whether as undersecretary or as cook—to create an organization and local associations. "I will empower them," she says. Based on the percentage of women who cast their votes at the polling station she supervised, Renee estimates that 70 percent of the population may now be women, and most of them are facing tremendous problems, particularly poverty. "The impact on improving the quality of life for those women is almost nil." In November 1993, she went as a delegate from the Khmer Women's Association, which she helped found, to the Asia-Pacific Symposium for Nongovernmental Organizations (NGOs) on Women in Development. Yet, Renee says, "the national urgent need is not the money but the unity, the real willingness and honesty to work together for the benefit of the country. Unity comes from trust. When you have trust you have unity, when you have unity you can do anything."

Renee is working even harder now that UNTAC has left, the elections are over, and the constitution has been changed. At the beginning of 1994, she was managing a technical staff of a hundred people who are setting up the National Computing Center for Cambodia. As well as doing the monthly payroll for 300,000 government employees, it will train local people in using, repairing, and setting up computers. "One side of the country is still in the stone age," she says, "and the other side is in the information age."

Extracts from her letters to friends reflect the challenges. June: "Fear still haunts many people. We need wisdom to conquer the ignorance. Sometimes I asked myself, can the nonviolence exist in the midst of violence?" July: "Getting to know each other does not yet exist. We need to build up bridges. We need constant dialogue in many ways." August: "What we have done so far seems not much compared with the vast destruction done by men exploiting until nothing is left. Nowadays I work tirelessly, never have a dull time. I use up all of my energy during the day and charge it up at night. My weekends are used by the local associations. The local people are eager to work to help others, despite having nothing but a commitment to shape up their family structure, which was fragmented by war. Everything is picking up slowly at the government level."

At times of stress, Renee turns to her quiet times, which give her inspiration to solve specific problems, and to meditation, when all the senses are at rest. "Meditation helps me to control my anger, my hatred, my greed, at a speed faster than the speed of light." It helps her avoid the trap of living in the past. Prayer, too, relaxes her mind and gives her a strong commitment to Buddhist teaching.

The country faces serious national problems with political infighting, corruption, and poverty; one child in five dies before the age of five; there are forty thousand amputees in need of rehabilitation; seven million land mines hold up development work and agricultural production. Robert Seiple, U.S. president of World Vision, an NGO which is helping in Cambodia, cautioned after an October 1993 visit against underestimating the national trauma of the last twenty years: Religion has been suppressed, families destroyed, and the values holding society together are greatly strained. "A very fragile infrastructure keeps this people intact," he says.

Renee is a valuable part of that infrastructure, a pillar of strength and integrity. She says, "Only God knows what I am doing; so far he is behind the whole thing. I can see the door is opening and the path is there. But the situation is not stable yet." In 1984, a group of Buddhist monks made an appeal from a refugee camp on the Thai-Cambodian border: "Cambodia has lost everything as a result of its long hostilities. We lost land, lives, and Buddhism. Our greatest loss is the ability to judge what is right and what is wrong. Please help us to recover this power." The land has been recovered, and, with the help of women like Renee Pan, the power will surely be recovered as well.

5

THESE TERRIBLE TIMES

*An Eritrean writer works for human rights in
her newly independent country.*

"WOMAN," A HARSH VOICE CALLED, "line up
with your comrades, hands behind your back, facing the wall."

As she did so, members of the firing squad raised their rifles.

This is it, she thought, and said a short prayer: "Oh, Lord, give
me the courage to die bravely like so many of my people have, without screaming, or begging for mercy, and receive me in thy Kingdom."

She heard the clicks of the guns being cocked and then, after
what seemed like an hour, "One, two, three," and her mind went
blank.

She opened her eyes. The guns were still pointed at their heads.
The officer said, "For anybody willing to confess, I will count up to
fifty." She counted with him. At fifty, he shouted, "Fire."

She heard the singing of birds and looked up. The sky was more
beautiful than she had ever known it. They were still alive. Her
inner voice said, "Be still, and you will be okay."

Two hours later the prisoners were ordered back to the cells. It
had been a ruse by her captors to try to extort information.

Abeba Tesfagiorgis had come a long way from her comparatively comfortable life in a two-story, cream-colored Italian villa in a beautiful suburb of Asmara, capital of Eritrea. Her story is "for everyone to whom freedom and justice are not negotiable," says Basil Davidson, author of *African Civilization Revisited.*

After World War II, Eritrea—which had been an Italian colony from 1890 and then under British rule for ten years—was incorporated in a loose federation with Ethiopia. But in 1961, Ethiopia annexed the region, and the people of Eritrea began their war for independence. They first had to battle a U.S.-supported regime in Ethiopia headed by Emperor Haile Selassie, then a Soviet-sponsored military *Dergue* (a Marxist junta) led by Colonel Mengistu Haile Mariam. It became Africa's longest war, dragging on for thirty years, with fifty thousand killed, many tortured, and nearly a third of the population of three million forced to flee. Every Eritrean family suffered losses.

As a high school student, and one of thirteen girls among the 350 pupils in the Prince Mekonnen Secondary School, Abeba had participated in student demonstrations against Ethiopian rule. The students protested the banning of the Tigrigna language and books and the imposition of the Amharic language, the language of the Ethiopian ruling ethnic group. "We students used to be furious as to why Ethiopia had a direct control of our sea and airports during federation," she says. "For any average Eritrean at the time, it was clear that Ethiopian rule meant nothing but destruction. That is the time that Eritrean independence became important to me."

Abeba attended the Haile Selassie University Extension in Asmara and studied sociology, accounting, and English. In 1961, she joined Ethiopian Airlines as administrative secretary to the district manager. It was the haggard faces of mothers who starved themselves to feed their children and the countless boys and girls with ashen lips who streamed through the Ethiopian Airlines office looking for jobs that made her join the underground movement of the Eritrean People's Liberation Front (EPLF). "There was no way to fight the evil government but by joining the EPLF," she says. She was a member of an underground cell at Ethiopian Airlines that met twice a week to read and discuss EPLF's newsletter, contribute money, and encourage others to form cells, each with no more than seven members. She secretly brought together the *tegadelti*, the freedom fighters, with other Eritreans.

During this period, Abeba wrote two novels in the Tigrigna language, *Woi Ane Dekai* (My Poor Children, 1969) and *Nemenye Zenegro* (Who Am I Going to Tell, 1974). They were fact-based and spoke of the social evils in the country—corruption, unemployment, the suffering of women, and the moral decadence of young and old. She was always more interested in reducing human suffering and tragedy than getting involved in politics. To this day she does not know how the books passed the censors. "There must have been a divine protection," she says. "These two books did good to my soul, for I was able to pour my heart into them. It is ugly not to have any right to almost everything, and it is uglier when you cannot do or say anything about it."

As cofounder and for six years chairperson of the Eritrean YWCA based in Asmara, she had helped develop classes in economics, dressmaking, first aid, and reading and writing; she also organized conferences on women and social problems, which took her to many countries. In 1974, as many of the country's villages were ravaged by war and drought, she turned her attention to the needs of the farmers and founded the Relief and Rehabilitation Association of Eritrea. She obtained permission to distribute grain, milk, and blankets. But the government became alarmed at the way the program was bringing people together and creating a sense of community, so it shut down the program, and Abeba had to continue clandestinely.

It was just as well that the Ethiopians only suspected but could not prove the extent of her involvement with the underground. On September 29, 1975, tipped off by an informer, two khaki-clad members of the *afagn* (the secret police), abducted her at gunpoint from the airlines office, forced her into a car, and drove her to the Palace Prison, where she was shoved into a windowless six-foot by five-foot cell with five other women. As the heavy iron door slammed shut behind her, she was consumed with anger. She was in another world, yet only ten minutes from her home. She was to spend six months as a prisoner, much of the time under the threat of execution.

Abeba's days in the cell were an education for her as she got to know the other women and their lives. Many of their experiences were foreign to her more sheltered existence, and there were terrible pressures put on them to incriminate their friends. Some of them had broken under the pressure and informed on others, and the atmosphere of bitterness and blame in the cell was intense. One evening after the traditional Coptic Orthodox prayer for forgiveness, Abeba said to the other women, "We all pray together for our release and for peace. But God will not answer our prayers if we keep on nursing resentment and hatred for one another." After a quick reaction and another violent exchange, the cell became enveloped in almost total silence. In the silence, Abeba thought that she should tell the women the story of Irene Laure, a Frenchwoman she had met at a conference in Asmara in 1969.

After describing Madame Laure's history and her willingness to open her heart to Germany despite all that she had been through, Abeba said, "My dears, it would be a disservice to our heroic *tegadelti* who fall in battle, to the mothers who suffer in silence the loss of their husbands and children, to our children who die pot-bellied due to malnutrition, to our pregnant women whose stomachs were slit with a sword and their stillborns tossed in the air, to our men who go off to work and never make it home, to the children whose limbs are hacked off by the enemy, to all those whose lives are a constant nightmare—it would be a disservice to all—if we did not forgive and love one another." She told them that just as Madame Laure could not hope to see a united and peaceful Europe without Germany, they could not say that they loved their country and then refuse to understand and forgive fellow Eritreans.

Soon after that, Abeba was brought face-to-face in the prison with the man who had betrayed her, and she realized that she had to practice what she preached, so she forgave him. "Hard as it was for me to forgive this contemptible informer, I made the decision that I would do so. I made it brief: 'That morning you shamelessly testified against me on just hearsay as a committed underground member of the EPLF, I hated your guts. Now I forgive you. If it were not for these horrendous times, neither you or I, or any of our cellmates, would be here in prison.'"

All sorts of pressures were brought to bear on Abeba to get her to confess, including the mock execution. Fortunately, she was not physically tortured like some of her cellmates were. But again she was told that she was to be executed and was even permitted to phone her husband, Mesfun, to ask him to bring her a Bible. "Life without you has no meaning for me," said Mesfun. "I will send you the Bible, but I want you to know that family and friends everywhere are praying for your release." After Mesfun tried to enlist the help of the U.S. vice-consul on behalf of his wife, he too was arrested by the governor and dragged off to prison.

By extraordinary coincidence, Abeba's own cell door was open as he was brought to the cell opposite, and they were able to embrace. "It's okay," whispered Mesfun, "just stick to what you have been saying. You have no confession to make. I see this as a God-given opportunity—how else could I have seen you? After all these weeks of grief and loneliness, now I can hold you in my arms. Continue to be brave and we shall come out together. Don't worry about the children—they are doing just fine in the care of their grandparents."

Abeba writes, "My cellmates were sobbing when I was thrown back to them. It must have been a pathetic sight—the reunion of a husband and wife, not in the privacy of their own home but in the corridor of a prison under armed guard and in the shadow of death."

For a time, Abeba's father was held in the prison as well. But having failed through threats of violence against her family to get a confession out of her, the authorities let her husband and father leave the prison. At the end of March 1976, unable to prove her guilt and being pressured from outside by different churches, including her own Coptic church, the government released Abeba. She was sent straight out of Eritrea to Ethiopia. In Addis Ababa, however, the situation was becoming more frightening; the communist "Red terror" meant more and more executions. So Abeba and Mesfun decided that it was time to leave.

Mesfun, who worked for the U.S. consulate, was able to get out by attending a seminar in Nairobi. Abeba, with their daughters, went via Asmara. With the help of an uncle in the EPLF and under the guise of attending a wedding, they escaped to a liberated area. Here, to her consternation, the two older daughters, Ruth and Tamar, decided to stay and fight with the EPLF. It would be eight years before she would have an emotional reunion with them in a Resistance camp, where they lived in underground bunkers. One would then be partially blind from a battle wound.

Abeba went on with her two younger daughters, Muzit and Senait, to the Sudan and Britain, eventually joining up with Mesfun in the United States, where her sisters lived. Like Renee Pan, Abeba Tesfagiorgis became a refugee in the United States. It was not easy. She had hoped to be able to bring their country's plight to the attention of the United Nations, but she failed to do so. "I felt completely helpless, devastated, that you had to be somebody, to have an office, power, to get any attention."

She was assailed by homesickness, and was worried about the daughters she had left behind, her parents, her relatives, her friends, and her people in general. When big offensives took place constantly, when the EPLF incurred setbacks, when drought and famine occurred nearly every year, when the possibility of total extinction, as she put it, was ever present, "you can imagine how every sensible Eritrean, inside or outside of his home, felt." With all these worries, though, she was thankful to her Creator that she was sane and was able to raise her children.

Abeba and her husband had emotional and financial struggles. She worked successively as secretary of the Poultry and Egg Institute in Roslyn, Virginia; as sales representative of the World Trade Transport Company in Washington, D.C., and and as an administrative assistant with the World Bank. Then in 1982 the family moved to Texas and took over a grocery store, struggling to put it on a sound footing. There they helped organize the participation of the Eritrean emigré community in the Dallas International Bazaar.

In May 1991, the fighters of the Ethiopian Peoples Revolutionary Democratic Front launched an offensive against the Ethiopian occupation army in Eritrea, finally toppling the *Dergue*. More than

130,000 Ethiopian soldiers in Asmara—one soldier for every five Eritreans—was either killed in the war or forced to lay down arms in defeat. Eritrea became free, and for the first time in thirty years, the light blue flag of Eritrea flew over the main buildings of Asmara, along with the red, green, and blue flag of the EPLF.

Abeba, like her fellow countrymen and -women the world over, rejoiced: "I used to ponder how we won this David-Goliath war. It was not because we had outside help, nor was it because we had the best warriors. It was because the *tegadelti* were selfless, highly motivated, and committed and caring. And the whole Eritrean population was behind them, supporting, helping, encouraging, and utterly collaborating." To every Eritrean, she says, it was like a second birth.

She decided to write a book to describe her people's struggle. In 1992, *A Painful Season and a Stubborn Hope: The Odyssey of an Eritrean Mother* was published. It chronicled the sacrifice and suffering of the women of the independence struggle as well as their incredible readiness to forgive, which she believes gives hope of a different direction for the continent.

Thomas Keneally, the Australian author of *Schindler's List*, said that as far as the rest of the world knew, her story might have been acted out on the dark side of the moon: "Her record of her experience at the hands of the Ethiopians in Asmara, and the odyssey which follows her escape from the hands of the torturers, gives us a picture of how thoroughly the forces of the Emperor, and then of the Stalinist dictator, Mengistu, alienated the Eritrean people. Abeba's voice is simply one voice raised on behalf of humanity and directed against the folly of dictators. Abeba's tale will astound, elevate and ennoble all who read it."

Abeba returned from exile in the United States to help found the Center for Human Rights and Development in Asmara. She does not hate the Ethiopians, but believes that it was often as much of a nightmare for the Ethiopian guards as it was for the prisoners. She says simply, "It was just these terrible times."

The April 1993 election, which legitimized Eritrea's independence from Ethiopia, was a time of jubilation, with thousands out in the streets. In a turnout of 98.5 percent of the approximately 1.1

Abeba Tesfagiorgis at the home of exile artist Solomon Tseggai Teferri in Montreal in 1991. Photograph by Teferri.

million registered voters, 99.8 percent voted in favor of independence. UN officials confirmed that the election was "free and fair." She believes that her people regarded it as a way of honoring those who died. "Those people who have voted freely all their lives may not take time to appreciate it."

Abeba believes that those same qualities of selflessness, commitment, and caring that helped win the war despite every kind of difficulty are needed if Eritrea is to reap the fruit of its hard-won independence and be a hope for Africa and an example for the world. Healing and development, she says, do not come as fast as destruction and death. "Of course, it is going to take us some time. But I am proud to say that the peace and tranquility we have is great."

The purpose of the Center for Human Rights and Development is to undertake education, research, communication, and advocacy to help societies in Eritrea and the Horn of Africa protect and promote human rights and attain social and economic development. Established as an independent, nonpartisan, nonprofit, nongovernmental institute, it is a civic organization that will work closely with many sectors of the public to help people learn more about their rights and responsibilities.

"After all this misery and pain, it is heaven to be free as a people and a nation. Every morning I thank my Creator for being alive, for coming back to my home where I was raised and had my kids, where my ancestors are buried. I can see my role and my fellow Eritrean women's role in building this small nation that has suffered so much for so long." Now that she has peace of mind and is looking at things with a new eye, she is also aware how much she loves the United States, which she describes as her second home.

Eritrea, a new nation that brings together Christians and Muslims from nine tribes, is, according to Dan Connell, American author of *Against All Odds—A Chronicle of the Eritrean Revolution*, "a bold, original experiment in cultural and political pluralism that promises to break ground in the effort to make democracy work in Africa" (*Christian Science Monitor*, April 30, 1993). It came into existence without major debts, financial or otherwise. The nationalist movement spent twenty-two months before independence working without pay and with little external aid to rebuild the country's devastated infrastructure—constructing farms and dams and reforesting barren hillsides. It is remarkably free of corruption. In 1992, thanks to good rains, new government initiatives, and peace, there was a fourfold increase in agricultural output. At the end of December 1993, however, the UN Food and Agriculture Organization reported that, because of the absence of rain, 70 percent of the year's harvest had failed. Eritrea will need massive amounts of aid to offset this unexpected setback and make swift economic strides if it is to maintain the enthusiasm with which the country was born. But it also needs more, Abeba believes.

In July 1993, she was asked to give the keynote address at a Symposium on Regional Cooperation in the Horn of Africa in Addis Ababa. The emphasis was on healing and reconstruction, and the title of her address was "From Conflict to Concord." One of her themes was that peace and development go hand in hand. It was a chance for her to put her deepest convictions before the distinguished audience, and it drew from them a wholehearted response.

The absence of war does not mean that there is peace, she told them. "If people of responsibility have wars in their hearts, which includes jealousy, vindictiveness, hunger for power, corruption, unforgiveness, lack of love for fellow human beings, and lack of wisdom, the battle to acquire peace, stability, and prosperity is only half won."

She challenged the politicians and government representatives to use their education not to boost their egos but to benefit others: "Use your status to serve others. Diplomacy, fine talks, and sophistication do not help. Simplicity and humbleness do. People who cheat their mates, who would do anything to keep their positions forever, who do not feel the pain of others, who do not put themselves into other people's shoes, who are not tolerant of opposition, are a menace to society.

"Let us get rid of our enemies not by imprisoning or killing them, as many African regimes are known to do, not by belittling them or humiliating them, but by resolving the conflict.

"With my country, Eritrea, having its independence after thirty long years of bitter armed struggle, with the new administration here in Ethiopia, with the standing committee, which is trying to do something about Somalia's predicament, with societies in the Horn being more and more conscious about regional cooperation, there is hope for a better future and resolving conflicts.

"Let us clean the garbage in our hearts. Let accountability be first to our conscience. It is not only the government that should be held responsible, but the people as well. Mengistu did not pull the trigger that killed the Ethiopian youth during the Red terror. He used people who deadened their consciences. They could have said, 'No, we are not going to kill our children,' but in the name of the government they did kill them.

"I do not expect every African to get rich soon. But I do expect in the very near future for all of us Africans to have basic necessities—enough food to eat and a hut that protects us from rain and heat. Let governments, civil institutions, and individuals have the vision and initiative to eradicate ignorance, famine, war, poverty, and take off the pain and the shame from the African."

Calling for a minute's silence for the martyrs who fell in battle to bring peace and dignity to Eritrea, Ethiopia, the Horn, and the whole continent, Abeba concluded her speech by quoting from a speech given by Abraham Lincoln just before the end of the Civil War: "With malice toward none, with charity for all, with firmness in the right as God gives us to see the right, let us strive on to finish the work we are in, to bind up the nation's wounds, to care for him who shall have borne the battle, and for his widow and his orphan, to do all which may achieve and cherish a just and lasting peace among ourselves and with all nations."

6

PINK ENVELOPES

A former Japanese senator still thinks for her country at age ninety-five.

BORN JUST AHEAD OF THE twentieth century, Shidzue Kato has often been ahead of her countrymen and -women as well. She is, writes Professor Barbara Molony, "one of the two or three most influential women in Japan's twentieth century history."

According to *The Japan Times* (August 9, 1992), "The life of Joan of Arc, the French heroine who led the French Army to victory in 1429, changed Kato eighty years ago from a coddled daughter of a noble samurai family to a brave woman deeply concerned about social problems." The paper quotes Shidzue: "I was so impressed to learn that a peasant girl rescued her country, because Japanese women were forced to be obedient to their husbands and only to do housework at that time. Thanks to her, I realized I could also contribute somehow to society." In that 1992 article headed "Age won't slow activist down," the paper wrote, "A passion for taking action to improve social conditions is still burning in Shidzue Kato, an influential feminist at the age of 95."

The year before, at the age of ninety-four, she expressed to the Japanese emperor and empress her gratitude for their visits to

Thailand, Malaysia, and Indonesia and their capacity to "sympathize with the pain felt by others." This is something Shidzue had been able to do over her lifetime, and in her message to the royal couple she referred to her own apology many years before at an international assembly "as a Japanese apology for what happened during the war."

Shidzue's father, Ritaro Hirota, was born in 1865, two years before the beginning of the Meiji Restoration, and studied mechanical engineering. This was the period when Japan was transformed from feudalism and the rule of the shogun (the general) to a more modern society. Ritaro could not afford expensive books, so he copied from cover to cover the whole volume of a Chinese-English dictionary that he needed. He was, as Shidzue once wrote, "A samurai not with the sword girded at his side, but with the engineer's rule in his pocket." Shidzue's mother had attended a Canadian mission school in Tokyo, so Shidzue benefited through both parents from exposure to foreign ideas and other cultures. Ritaro returned home from his travels abroad with furniture, pianos, cameras, sewing machines, and children's clothes. The parents were also in touch with the foremost Japanese reformers of the day. "I was impressed by stories of those who had done great things, both Japanese and foreign," says Shidzue. "I felt I must become a woman who did something good."

Although Western trained and outwardly modern, Shidzue's father was run by the feudal code of the old regime. Shidzue was brought up in a purely Japanese fashion, attending the exclusive Peeresses' School. She writes of the entry of five-year-olds to the kindergarten: "Little boys and girls of aristocratic birth were brought to this kindergarten carefully protected by their servants, some wrapped in soft silk quilts and riding on the nurses' knees in the *rikishas*, as if their parents were afraid even a soft wind might kill their little ones."

At the start of the Meiji era, all Japanese had been declared by law to be equal, and monogamy was fixed as the foundation of the moral code. But by the time Shidzue awakened to social consciousness, only three decades had passed since these new laws had taken effect and there was almost no understanding, she says, of the "actual meaning of equality."

Three weeks after graduation, an arranged marriage with Baron Keikichi Ishimoto was proposed to her. She liked what she was told of him and agreed. He was ten years older than she was and had a wide knowledge of East and West. He had written his graduation thesis in English and read the Chinese classics as easily as his own language. He was also a Christian. He equaled her in determination to do something for society. Knowing that being a woman was a handicap and that she could not do much, Shidzue decided "to be the wife of someone who could."

As a mining engineer, he asked to be posted to the Miike coal mine in Kyushu. They lived there from 1915 to 1918, and her "heart ached," as she put it, to see the conditions in the pits, particularly for the women. These women had to do all the housework after working in the mines for more than twelve hours a day, even when they were pregnant. She and her husband both worked to improve conditions. As she watched the lives of these laborers and their women and children, the questions rose in her mind that "were to grow and revolutionize" her own life. Her first son was born there.

In 1919, her husband traveled to the United States to study social issues. Since he had no wish for there to be a great gap between her knowledge and his, he wanted her to join him as soon as she had finished nursing her second baby. He wrote to her, "Don't come abroad if you seek pleasure and new fashions in clothes or are planning to spend your time only at the theaters or motoring like other 'bourgeoises mesdames.' Come to me if you will educate yourself, to feed yourself with knowledge of the world, to prepare yourself to swim abreast the world's new tides."

On that first trip to the United States, she enrolled in a secretarial course, getting A's in stenography, bookkeeping, secretarial duties, and typewriting. But the most significant event of the tour was a meeting with Margaret Sanger, a visiting nurse in the New York slums. "Listening to her account of the birth-control movement, the memory of the overcrowded miners' huts in western

Japan came back so vividly that the idea of my true vision in life flashed over me. 'Yes, Mrs. Sanger's fight has to be fought in my country, too. I will carry the banner for birth control in Japan.'" She knew that she would have to cultivate courage to do so. "Japanese women had no concept of controlling their sex lives at that time, and poor women had more children than they could afford to raise. The moment I met her, I decided to bring the birth-control movement to Japan."

In the United States, her husband became disillusioned with what he felt were limits to Christian humanism, believing that its analysis was not radical enough. They both traveled to Europe and were struck by the effects of World War I. The failure of Christians to prevent the hatred prevailing between European nations weighed on them. Mountain climbing, says Shidzue, came as a relief to their spiritual agony. Despite those who tried to dissuade her because she was a woman, she climbed the Jungfrau with her husband.

She was faced with other mountains to scale on her return to Japan—the ramparts of tradition and convention. To gain some independence, she worked as a secretary with the YWCA; opened a yarn shop with a little school adjoining, where Western knitting was taught; and even published a book on knitting that sold thirteen thousand copies. In 1922, Shidzue hosted Margaret Sanger on her first visit to Japan.

A year later she felt sufficiently confident to emulate Sanger and stand before an audience to lecture on birth control. A young labor organizer, Kanju Kato, invited her to speak to the workers at a copper mine. He managed to fill the lecture hall, with each of the miners paying about half a day's wages to attend. Twenty years later they were to marry.

Shidzue's work at the front line of birth control was a cause of alarm to the authorities, and especially to people of her own class. She was caricatured in papers and magazines and dubbed "Madame Control." "On my return from travels in the Western countries I had broken the shackles of mean conventions little by little, had taken steps along the road to emancipation for myself and pointed the way for others, disregarding the social prejudices against independent action for a woman."

Weary in spirit, she visited the United States again in 1924. "Even my short stay in the United States restored my health and cleared away the gloom that had settled upon my spirit. The youthful democratic country worked like magic on the subject of an ancient state. I felt fresh energy springing up within me. I was ready once more for the battle at home."

She was also finding comfort in Buddhism. "On my religious pilgrimage I reached the goal of spiritual enlightenment not in Mecca nor in India but on the dusty bookshelves of my husband's library." She was inspired by a book about a thirteenth century sect founded by Nichiren, whose name was a synonym for brave action related to ideals. She responded to it because she saw it as "the religion of social righteousness requiring action under persecution and every difficulty." It was the only sect of Japanese Buddhism, she said, that declared the unfairness of ranking women below men. "My interest in Nichiren has to do with his spiritual strength and the courage which never failed him even when faced with the threat of death."

By the mid-1920s, established as one of Japan's leading authorities on birth control, Shidzue plunged into the battle for women to be enfranchised. She joined the Alliance of Suffragettes and was appointed chairperson of its finance committee. She spoke at meetings and, in 1927, mobilized support for a petition to the government. The reply to the petition from Home Minister Keisuke Mochizuki stated, "Go back to your home and wash your babies' clothes. That is the job given to you and there is the place in which you are entitled to sit." The home minister in the next government was more sympathetic. A bill was passed in the lower house of Parliament granting civil rights to women, only to be rejected by the House of Peers without serious discussion.

On a 1932–33 lecture tour of the United States, Shidzue renewed her association with Margaret Sanger and spoke at a convention in Chicago arranged by the National Council of Women. She was inspired by other speakers at the convention, including Carrie Chapman Catt, Jane Addams, and Margaret Bondfield. "I derived from them a stronger determination than ever to face the modern world courageously and as intelligently as possible."

Shidzue Kato typing the draft of Facing Two Ways *at her home in 1934. Photograph from the Kato collection.*

In 1932 she founded the Women's Birth Control League of Japan, and in 1934 she opened the nation's first clinic modeled on Sanger's New York clinic. Finding few birth-control devices available in Japan, she turned her kitchen into a laboratory for the manufacture and packaging of creams and jellies. At the time, the government was encouraging women to have as many children as possible to strengthen military power and provide a source of cheap labor.

In 1935, Shidzue's autobiography, *Facing Two Ways*, was published. She translated it into English and the book was on the American best-seller list. One historian described it as "the most graphic primary source in English of the dark side of the Meiji modernization." It was subsequently used as a text on Japanese social relations by Americans planning for the postwar occupation of the country.

Shidzue plunged more and more into women's issues. It was a difficult time, because the "militarists" were coming to power. They exercised "thought control" over anyone who was at variance with their thinking and with their perception of the traditional values of Japan. By 1937, she was under government surveillance as a purveyor of "dangerous thoughts," and her house was ransacked for evidence of seditious writings. At the end of the year, two thousand citizens were arrested—two of them women, one of them Shidzue. She was in prison for two weeks for "violating public order" and was then released. But her clinic was closed, and the confidential records of her clients were confiscated. "Birth control was not prohibited by law," she says, "but police arrested me because my cause ran counter to Japan's social climate; the government was desperate to strengthen economic and military power. But I never gave up trying to spread the birth-control movement, since I believed it would greatly help Japanese women."

The World War II years brought Shidzue much suffering. There was little food, her closest friends in the reform movement, including her future husband, were in jail; and because of her prewar trips to United States and her antiwar attitudes, her neighbors were keeping their distance. One son, Tamio, died of tuberculosis; the other, Arata, was drafted and, after refusing to take the officer candidate exam because of his antiwar beliefs, was shipped off to Sumatra as a truck driver. Eventually he was repatriated and became a university professor.

During the 1920s and 1930s, Shidzue's husband had lost his reforming zeal and had become absorbed in unsuccessful projects in Korea and Manchuria. In 1944, she divorced him because he devoted himself to the colonization of Manchuria, believing that it was the best way to help Japanese laborers. "I could not be his wife anymore. His deeds and thoughts were completely beyond my understanding." Later that same year, when she was 48, she married Kanju Kato, and the following year their daughter was born.

After the war, her work for birth control continued. In 1949, she hosted the first of several more visits by Margaret Sanger. In 1954, Sanger became the first American woman to speak before the Japanese Diet (Parliament). In the introduction to a new 1984 edition of *Facing Two Ways,* Professor Molony wrote, "Kato Shidzue's work in bringing Sanger's ideals to Japan had indeed succeeded in fundamentally changing Japanese society and politics" (p. xxviii). Birth control had given Japanese women "the freedom from biology that permits them to be employed, to be educated, to develop their interests, and to be politically involved."

In 1952, Shidzue served as the Japanese representative at the inaugural meeting of the International Planned Parenthood Federation in London. And fifty years after her arrest, she was chosen as the first Japanese recipient of the United Nations Population Award. In 1990, she was awarded the Avon Grand Award of one million yen for her seven-decade fight for the sexual and human rights of women. She was then chairperson of the Japan Family Planning Association and vice chairperson of the Foundation for International Cooperation in Family Planning.

The period since World War II added another facet to her life in Japan and in its outreach to the world. A new election law was promulgated by the occupation authorities, and Japanese women went to the polls for the first time on April 10, 1946. Two-thirds of the female electorate voted, and more than half of the women candidates were successful. Thirty-nine women entered the 1946 House of Representatives. Both Shidzue and Kanju, as Socialist candidates, won overwhelming victories, with Shidzue getting the highest majority in the country. She became a member of the House special committee charged with drafting a new constitution.

"The Meiji constitution, established in 1900, totally ignored women's rights," she says. Before World War II, Japanese wives did not even have the right to inherit property or divorce their husbands, even if the husbands kept mistresses. Japanese women could not attend public universities. "As a female Diet member, it was most important to establish the new constitution, which guarantees women's rights. Today's Japanese women are highly educated and know how to use their knowledge to improve the social condition. I believe they will play a key role in the twenty-first century."

Shidzue was also an advisor to General MacArthur on policies affecting women. After two terms in the lower House she was elected in May 1950 to the House of Councillors (the Senate), where she served four six-year terms and was a member of the Foreign Affairs Committee, retiring in 1974.

In 1951, Senator Kato attended an MRA (see p. 171) assembly in the United States. The atmosphere was different from that of international meetings she had attended before the war. There was talk of a change in people being the basis for a change in society. At first, she thought that this notion was "nonsense." But then she decided to deal with things in her own life that needed to be different. "It was almost like the funeral of an arrogant woman," she says. On her return to Japan, she was so different that at first her husband did not recognize her at the airport. One of the first things she did was to apologize to her stepdaughter. "I used to train her, but I didn't love her," she said. She wrote a letter of apology, and they became "like a real mother and daughter." She began to develop new attitudes and ideas in her work and was able to clear up a rivalry that had separated her from another Diet member in her own party.

In 1957, she was invited to another assembly at Baguio, the summer capital of the Philippines. It was a chance for her to work on improving relations with Southeast Asian neighbors. With her at Baguio was Niro Hoshijima, chairman of the Japan-Korea Society. With the permission of Japanese Prime Minister Nobosuke Kishi, Hoshijima launched exploratory talks with Koreans, hoping to solve the problems that existed between the two countries.

Before World War II, Japan had occupied Korea for thirty-six years, controlling every aspect of its life and even forbidding the speaking of Korean. In 1957, no Japanese citizen was allowed to enter Korea. A 1953 statement about Japan's postwar claims in Korea made by chief Japanese delegate Kanichiro Kubota at a conference on Korean-Japanese relations was a particular irritant.

At Baguio, the Japanese apologized to the Koreans for Japan's behavior over the years. The Japanese daily *Yomiuri Shimbun* headlined its report describing the informal talks between the Japanese and Koreans, "Beginnings of a solution to the Japanese-Korean problem." It referred to the response in Korea to the apology and said that a telegram had reportedly been sent by members of government and opposition parties in Korea to the effect that this action brought hope of the dawning of a new day in Japanese-Korean talks.

Yoong Sung Soon, chairman of the Foreign Relations Committee of the Korean National Assembly, said that anti-Japanese feeling was running high because of bitter experiences, but "through Mr. Hoshijima and Mrs. Kato we have fortunately been able to learn of Japan's good faith." After the talks with the Koreans, Hoshijima and Kato came to the conclusion that if the Japanese government would first issue a statement retracting the Kubota declaration and renounce property claims, the way would be opened for a possible resolution of the various issues.

In a subsequent debate in the Japanese Parliament, Senator Kato spoke of the Baguio conference and, in particular, of how the Japanese and Korean representatives had "established feelings of trust without diplomatic tactics." "We Japanese learned how much the Korean people suffered under the Japanese rule for more than thirty years. Feelings in Koreans' hearts will not be resolved overnight. At Baguio we Japanese deeply apologized and admitted our wrongdoings, and Koreans opened their hearts. Mr. Hoshijima and I promised that on our return we would put our best effort, above party, into tackling the basic difficulties in the deadlocked negotiations."

Replying to a question from the senator, Prime Minister Kishi said, "I agree wholeheartedly with Mrs. Kato on all she has said about Korean-Japanese relations. The most important point in our negotiations is not the interpretation of laws and rights but, as Mrs. Kato has said, to give priority to the creation of the right spirit between our countries. We on our side must take the initiative."

Dealing with the two issues to which Korea had most strongly objected, the prime minister said, "I have no hesitation in withdrawing the Kubota statement. I regret that it has given Korea the impression of our people's feeling of superiority." Referring to Japanese property claims in Korea, Kishi said, "I have no intention of holding to our past legal interpretations." He added, "From now on, as far as Japan is concerned, we should not hold to our past assertions but try fairly to solve these many practical issues on the basis of a humble heart."

That autumn, Prime Minister Kishi, responding to his country's need for new markets for its expanding industry, decided to make a diplomatic tour through seven countries in Southeast Asia and through Australasia. Basil Entwistle, in his book, *Japan's Decisive Decade*, recounts a conversation he had at the time with Senator Kato and Yukika Sohma (see Chapter 10):

> "We feel it is unrealistic," said Yukika, "for him to go around Asia talking about trade without first trying to open people's hearts. There's far too much bitterness for them to be willing to enter into business deals."
> "What do you think he should do?" asked Entwistle.
> "Well, we saw at Baguio we wouldn't have got anywhere without humbly apologizing for the past," said Shidzue. "If Kishi really wants to normalize relations with Southeast Asia, he'd better begin the same way." (p. 169)

Questioned by Entwistle whether the prime minister would be willing to go on the record, Shidzue replied, "When I talked with him about Korea I think he was sincere in recognizing the need for Japan to make restitution, and he went ahead and withdrew the Kubota statement over the protest of the bureaucrats."

She sought the assistance of Hoshijima, who had become speaker of the House of Representatives, and between them, Entwistle records, the groundwork was laid for what was afterwards dubbed "the statesmanship of the humble heart." "Shidzue was able to open the door for the Prime Minister to indicate publicly his desire to redeem the past. Despite the protests of bureaucrats, Kishi insisted that his prepared speeches be rewritten."

Calling on the prime minister, Shidzue offered him the support of the opposition if, before discussing trade relations, he would first express the sincere apologies of the Japanese people for the wrongs of the past. "The economic future of Japan," she said, "depends as much on trust as on trade."

According to Garth Lean in *On the Tail of a Comet*, "Kishi heeded Mrs. Kato's advice when he went to the Philippines, Korea, Burma, and finally Australia" (p. 497). The *Sydney Morning Herald*

Shidzue Kato in 1981 with former Prime Minister Nobosuke Kishi whom she challenged to put apology before trade. Photograph from the Kato collection.

(December 5, 1957) wrote: "We cannot afford the luxury of living in the bitter past . . . . Kishi handled a delicate mission with skilful tact. His ice-breaking tour . . . could hardly have been a pleasant experience. But no one could have gone further in making official amends for the sins of his country."

Reporting afterwards, the *Washington Evening Star* (December 18, 1957) wrote: "Premier Kishi is now back in Tokyo after having completed one of the most unusual missions ever undertaken by a statesman of his rank. Over the past three weeks he has visited no fewer than nine nations that Japan occupied or threatened with conquest . . . and in each of these lands he publicly apologized for his country's actions during the war."

On the last day of 1957, a preliminary declaration on the terms of a settlement between Japan and Korea was signed.

As an opposition member, Senator Kato had not held back from helping Kishi heighten his concept. Nor was she hesitant about standing up to elements in her own party when she believed that the health of Japanese democracy was threatened. This happened in 1960, when the question of renewal of the Security Treaty with the United States came up. The parties were divided, relations with the United States were imperiled, and communism threatened to gain from the violence that ensued. In statements that appeared widely in newspapers and on television, Senator Kato helped underline for the nation the kind of society that Japan should have. She worked for a settlement on the basis of *what* was right rather than *who* was right. She appealed for her own Socialist party to change from violence, ambition, and class war to unity and moral straightness. The choice, she said, was between a violent revolution from without or a moral revolution from within.

In 1971, Senator Kato was in London just after Emperor Hirohito's visit to Britain and the Netherlands. She apologized to both countries for her country's actions in World War II. Japan, she said, had tried to restore peace after the war by adopting a peaceful way and giving money to help other nations, but it had not realized how much bitterness still remained in people's hearts. BBC Radio News called her remarks a sequel to the royal visit and quoted her statement that the emperor's visit was worthwhile because many of the British people accepted and welcomed him.

"What we did was wrong, and what was wrong must be admitted and put right between nations as well as individuals if we are to build trust," she said in an interview broadcast over Dutch television. Thirty-eight former Dutch prisoners in Japanese camps in Indonesia responded with an open letter in which they stated, "This lady who did not justify but who honestly admitted guilt and who asked the Netherlands to accept her apologies, will help us all to leave the past behind, with all its feelings of hatred and revenge, in order to create better relations with the people of Japan."

In 1975, Kato retired from the Senate and, after her husband's death in 1978, left the Socialist party so that she could speak more freely. "Too often people are controlled by a company or other loyalty," she said. She was asked to appear regularly on television, commenting on political developments. NHK, the national television company, produced a forty-five-minute documentary highlighting her work for women.

She says, "I try to make friends with people who do good work nationally and internationally. Old people living alone often feel unstable, but if you live alone you can do anything! I have a daily time of quiet when I feed my spiritual life, and this is the secret of my energy."

For some years it has been her habit to send letters in pink envelopes to people who are pursuing some worthy cause that benefits Japanese society. Since 1987 she has sent fifty of these pink missives. The first recipient was Hajime Tamura, former minister of international trade, for his swift action in apologizing to the United States for an export violation by a Japanese manufacturer. Other recipients have ranged from an employee of a convenience store to former Prime Minister Toshiki Kaifu, whom she encouraged because of his campaign against corruption in his cabinet.

"If people appreciate the efforts of others by sending letters," she says, "those who have received letters will be encouraged to do some other good things again. This kind of gesture will prompt people to behave in the right way." She plans to start sending her pink letters to people overseas. "I am ninety-five years old, but still curious to do something for society and women," she says.

She sees Japan becoming a big power economically but becoming poorer and poorer spiritually. "We must try to stop this slide," she says. "Many point to Japan and China as world leaders in the twenty-first century. Japan must take responsibility for the welfare and prosperity of the world."

7

HEALING HISTORY

*A Bostonian works to heal the history with
which she is a link.*

*An African American wishes to be midwife to
a new generation.*

IN 1993, EDITH STATON WAS named as a consult-
ant to a new committee for curing racial bias at her integrated Epis-
copal church in Cambridge, Massachusetts. The appointment
would not be surprising except for the fact that she was then ninety-
seven years old. The position is a tribute not to her longevity but to
her faithfulness to the task of trying to build a prejudice-free United
States. She keeps on top of the news, eagerly questions visitors, and
continues to work in the campaigns of those political candidates
she supports. She got the residents in her apartment block into
recycling before the city took it up. And when she was phoned early
one morning to check a fact for this book, she was already out. In a
church raffle she had offered her services to clean someone else's
silver, and that is what she was doing!

Edith is one of a growing number of American women and men
who believe that an important step in curing racial bias is an honest
conversation about the past. Through mutual forgiveness, those
whose people suffered and those whose people may have been
responsible for the suffering can find productive ways of working

together. She identifies strongly and courageously with the latter group. She feels an urgency about healing the hurts of American history and she is a living link with that history.

Edith was born in Blair House in Washington, D.C., in 1896. Then the family home, it is now the official state guest house, and she was the last child born there. When she was still a small child, the family moved to the Blair family farm in Silver Spring, Maryland, so named because her great-grandfather, Francis Preston Blair, discovered a spring in the woods while out riding.

Her grandfather, Montgomery Blair, was the lawyer who argued the famous Dred Scott case before the U.S. Supreme Court during 1856–57. Her grandfather lost the case for Scott's freedom, but Edith is proud that he based his argument on the point that slaves were human beings and not property. Montgomery Blair later became postmaster general in Abraham Lincoln's cabinet.

During the Civil War one of Edith's aunts, Minna Blair Richey, was part of a riding party with the president just north of Washington when they found themselves too close to Confederate troops and had to take shelter in the only fort on the north side of the city, Fort Stevens. Southern general, Jubal Early, had brought his troops around north of Washington for a surprise attack. Aunt Minna remembered President Lincoln peeping out over the stockade to get a glimpse of the Confederates and a young aide pulling his coattails to keep him down. Years later, this incident was corroborated in the memoirs of that aide, Oliver Wendell Holmes.

The Confederate soldiers came across the Blair farm. The officers at one house found the whiskey, while the men at the other managed to set the home on fire with their campfires. Edith's father, Montgomery Blair, Jr., used to say that it was the Blair whiskey that saved Washington.

The house was eventually rebuilt, and Edith's family went there to live around the turn of the century. After the Fort Stevens battle, the body of a Confederate soldier was found near the spring and was buried by the woods with a small stone marker. "As children, we used to put violets on the grave every spring," says Edith. She was one of seven children. They had a black maid, Dee, who also

Edith Staton, whose grandfather was in Lincoln's cabinet, with her own great-granddaughter. Photograph by John P. McCabe.

looked after the children. She had been born a slave in North Carolina. "We loved her," says Edith. "She stayed with us until she died. But she never sat at table with us. She didn't expect it, and neither did we."

Edith says that only after she began to take time in quiet to seek direction was she able to have an honest conversation in her own spirit about the past and to face the depth of racial bias in herself. "I realized that as much as I loved [Dee], there was a difference; we never ate together. I have begun to see that I have an inborn racial prejudice that is deep-rooted. But I do believe that we can pray for forgiveness for all kinds of sins, and it does come. It's like an alcoholic; until you admit that you have a racial bias, you can't be helped to change."

Edith's husband was Adolphus Staton, a navy admiral who died in 1964. Her father-in-law had run away from home, a southern plantation, at the age of fifteen to join the Confederate army. Later in life he would say that he was glad that the South had lost, because slavery was terrible for the owners as well as the slaves. It fed a false pride and attitude of superiority which, says Edith, "has descended to the third and fourth generations."

Such attitudes and low expectations of blacks are a source of deep regret for Edith. She is particularly concerned about the legacy of slavery in terms of the needs of inner-city schools and what she regards as the selfishness of wealthy suburbs. "Integrating the schools has been an important step," she says, "but the inner schools need equitable funding with suburban schools. The people who need things most, help with education and social services, get the least. This is wrong. We're all responsible for the whole community. If you live in the suburbs you cannot ignore the plight of the inner city."

The future of inner-city children is at the top of the agenda of Audrey Burton, an African American living in Richmond, Virginia. She calls herself "a midwife giving birth to a new generation of African-American children, rescuing them from a hostile environment." Audrey was born in New Orleans, Louisiana, on December 31, 1939. Her grandfather on her father's side lived until he was almost a hundred and was partly of native American descent, or, as he put it, from the "Indian clan"; his mother was French and white. Audrey's mother was a domestic and a presser in a laundry, and her father was a minister and a laborer. She grew up in a home where values and faith in God were instilled by both parents. Religious language has always been Audrey's natural means of expression. "When God has something for me to do," she says, "He takes the kinks out of it." Or, "Wherever I am needed, the Lord will send me. Collie and I will go and take care of the Lord's business." That readiness has taken her and her husband to Zimbabwe and to India, to the prison system in the United States and now to caring for the younger generation of African Americans.

Audrey characterizes her years growing up as happy ones, though the family had few belongings and lived in a shotgun house with a tin roof and an outdoor privy. She lived in an all-black neighborhood, played on dirt sidewalks and dark streets with no lights, and attended all-black schools and an all-black church. She graduated from high school in 1958. After having earned enough money, she enrolled in a business college in 1960. She graduated with honors two years later and joined the faculty. It was clear, however, that teaching was not for her, and after applying for several secretarial positions, she started working with a small minority moving and storage firm. This was the time when she "began to see things as they really were." Positions were available, "but not to the darker skinned person like myself."

With the boom in the space industry that came in the early 1960s, she had an opportunity to join Chrysler, where she worked for five years. During that time she got married. In the late 1960s, however, she suffered some setbacks: cancer that required major surgery, the death of a sister, and separation and subsequent divorce from her husband. Just as she was beginning to feel that life was unfair, she was hired by the Urban League in her own city, New Orleans, at the start of 1970. She was launched into community work, where she learned a sensitivity toward people.

Later that year she moved to Richmond, Virginia, to marry Collie, a single father of three. She became involved in community work there too. Encountering racism, she tried to change attitudes as an office manager of an international labor union. She tried to change the policies of a national organization for professional secretaries that either denied African-American women membership or shunted aside those it did accept. Her confrontational approach had both positive and negative results, but she failed to resolve the situation and left in anger. "When it comes down to it, [confrontation] can be seen as a disservice," she says. But then she went on to encourage African-American women to form their own organization to enhance personal development.

A visit to Caux in 1982 with her husband introduced her to people from all over the world and to "new avenues to approach old situations." As a result, she became more tolerant and started reaching out to people who had different political views or came from other communities. "Before, I would have written people off, but when I practice standards of honesty, unselfishness, love, and purity, then I can be around almost anyone and it doesn't set off a time bomb. Most importantly, it's a matter of seeking God's guidance each day and following his direction." She discovered a desire to work for both parties involved in any confrontation.

It was her work as a community coordinator for a Catholic diocese that led her into the corrections field. She visited a client in prison to experience firsthand what went on there. "I wanted to see how a jail was operated. I couldn't imagine what was there. I didn't know if it was a calling or not. I believe it was a preparation for something larger." She worked for nine months with the city of Richmond jail system, then at the Virginia General Assembly, the state's Office of Public Safety and Transportation, and the Virginia Department of Corrections. When Allyn Sielaff, her boss there, became commissioner of the New York City Department of Correction in 1990, Audrey went with him to take up the newly created post of special assistant, specializing in community relations. Her husband, Collie, became director of administration for the Department's Nutritional Services Division.

In 1988, the Burtons went to India to participate in a *yatra*, a spiritual journey, honoring the 120th anniversary of the birth of Mahatma Gandhi and the link between him and the nonviolence of Martin Luther King, Jr. While in India, they were inspired by the Gandhian principles put forward at the Institute for Total Revolution and challenged by Gandhi's grandson, Rajmohan, to help complete the unfinished business of his grandfather's revolution. They met Gandhians who had spent time in prison and realized that these men and women had used prison as a means of strengthening their belief systems and their connections to God. Audrey recognized that "you can be locked away and still be a productive person in terms of your spiritual development."

She returned with the embryo of an idea that she was able to implement in New York. She was appalled at the high rate of repeat offenders—those released from the ten prisons on Riker's Island in the city's East River who committed other crimes and came back. People who had served sentences for drug possession and theft were returning to the same temptations on the streets; for many, life in prison—where at least basic needs were met—seemed a better alternative to life in the community. So Audrey decided to set up an Institute for Inner Development (IID) to try to break this cycle. "What we're trying to do," said Audrey, "is to wake people up and say look where you're at. Maybe if they know why they are here then they'll try to build up the community instead of trying to tear it down."

The philosophy of IID urges each individual to accept responsibility for his or her actions and sets out to build self-esteem. She drew on professionals from the African-American and Hispanic communities to lead empowerment sessions. The eight-week courses taught problem solving, decision making, anger management, and financial responsibility. She also developed IID community sites where graduates could be received when they were released from prison.

In IID's first years of operation, acts of violence in one correctional center were reduced by 50 percent. Out of seventy-five prisoners released from one of the institute's classes, only three were rearrested. There is a list of corrections officers who are eager for assignment to the program. One ex-prisoner wrote to the warden of the Otis Bantum Correctional Center on Riker's Island, "I'd like to thank you all for waking me up to reality and realizing there's still hope in life for individuals such as myself."

Audrey gives the credit to others and sees herself as a catalyst. "My colleagues and I spent endless hours talking about how we wanted to put things together. It was the ideas that poured out of people's brains that God put in place to give their piece of this puzzle. When you are doing something that is God-sent, rather than for your own self-gratification, you keep working at it, because there is a prize on the other end."

In 1993, Audrey returned to Richmond, but the work she started in New York continues. At the end of 1993, the institute was in full operation in four facilities, and the process had been recommended for implementation in all institutions.

In Richmond, Audrey has switched her focus from treatment to rescue, cure, and healing. She works with women who live in public housing, an after-school group, a group of adult males, and young people at a center for troubled youth, but her main emphasis—almost a new phase in her life—is her work with young school-age African Americans. She has a sense of urgency fueled by the

statistics, which she has at her fingertips from newspaper stories—
statistics that highlight the continuing seriousness of the problem:

- At the current rate of incarceration, at least half of all the
  young black men in America will be in prison or on parole by
  the year 2000.
- About 1.5 million black male teenagers will be dead or in
  prison before their thirtieth birthday.
- For every black teenager who goes to college, three will go to
  prison.
- Blacks constitute 13 percent of the urban population but
  account for more than half of those arrested for murder, rape,
  and nonnegligent manslaughter.
- From 1977 to 1982, more than half the juvenile arrests for
  the most violent crimes were among black teenagers, and the
  relative rate of incarceration for black and white youth was
  forty-four to one.

With these alarming figures in mind, Audrey developed a course
that she calls "a rescue program" for young people, a training in
moral and spiritual values modestly named "Social Graces and
Mini-Manners." It is a carefully thought-out program drawing on
her years of experience. She designed a training manual to address
the things that she has identified as priorities, such as the development of a positive self-image and the promotion of positive lifestyles
in a hostile environment. The program focuses on moral and spiritual training, effective living studies, image reconstruction, and self-
esteem so that young people can become responsible, dependable,
sincere individuals and make a major contribution to community
and world. Audrey wants them to "see themselves as beautiful, powerful, in God's creation." She adds, "Any child, man, or woman,
can use the manual to be changed."

In this context, three times a week she spends two hours with
sixth, seventh, and eighth graders at Elijah House Academy, a private school started by what she calls a couple of European descent
whose purpose was to "rescue " inner-city children. There are very
high expectations of good behavior from the youngsters and a

strong emphasis on discipline, honesty, and character. Required reading and visual material includes *Roots*, *The Civil War*, and *Eyes on the Prize* about the civil rights movement. To encourage serious thought on career goals, all the children make collages depicting what they want to do when they grow up. "I am striving for both inner and academic excellence," she says.

Like many others in today's civil rights battles, Audrey believes that the failure of the majority population to address the problem of what is happening to young blacks can only be attributed to what amounts to racism. At the same time, she says clearly to the young African Americans in her care, "I don't want you to blame white people for anything. We are working on a healing process here. I want you to be able to talk about yourself and not be ashamed. You identify and describe other people based on how you see yourself. My being a healer means that I am to help people understand who they are, their history, their culture, their spirituality and to seek out their role and at times to be willing to reject some things our parents have taught us."

"Healing" is a key word in Audrey's current preoccupations. In June 1993, a national cities conference was held in Richmond with the theme "Healing the Heart of America—An Honest Conversation on Race, Reconciliation, and Responsibility." The event, which mobilized the city, was the fruit of sustained work by a group of Richmonders over a long period. One of those providing leadership was Audrey. She felt that since she had begun a process of healing her own spirit, she might have something to contribute at such a conference. "As there was in me a buildup of pain, anxiety, and frustration caused by racism, by the way I had been socialized and shaped by society, I felt I had a part in healing other hearts. There had been a need in myself to release a drowning spirit, to open up the well so that I might get to the real spirit the Creator had for me. The process was like peeling away the skins of an onion. It is an encouragement that we can move from being an onion that makes you cry to becoming a sweet potato!"

Her involvement in the conference, she says, stemmed from the fact that the concept did not originate primarily among African Americans but among people of European descent who were bold

Audrey Burton at the "Healing the Heart of America" conference that she helped organize in Richmond, Virginia in 1993. Photograph by Rob Lancaster.

enough to take to heart the expressions of hurt, fear, and anxiety they heard from African Americans and to begin a serious process of bringing the issue to the forefront so that people could discuss it. What she does not say is that when some of those considering such a conference were tempted to draw back or water down the concept, her voice urged them to press ahead.

One feature of the conference was the Richmond Unity Walk, where Richmonders and those attending the conference walked through the city's history together, honoring the dead—both black and white—and the pain suffered by all races, whether it was the native Americans who first inhabited the area, the slaves who were landed at the Manchester docks, or the soldiers who fought and died for the Confederacy. Richmond Mayor Walter T. Kenney, who led the walk, said, "This city will never again be the same."

Audrey believes that the conference and the walk were unique. "Such an honest conversation on race has never before taken place in the United States on the spiritual level that characterized the Richmond process; up until then, race had been too often talked about on an intellectual level. The conference confirmed for me that rather than speak about racism, I am to speak about healing."

A video of the walk was made so that other cities might be inspired to undertake their own appropriate gestures to heal history. And up in Cambridge, one of the first people to buy the video was Edith Staton. She wants it, naturally, for her new committee for curing racial bias. "It is a first step in showing us where we are," she says.

In March 1994, the Richmond City Council unanimously established a Richmond Unity Walk Commission to establish the walk "as a permanent national educational resource, as a contribution to healing Richmond's racial history, and as an inspiration to all the people of this metropolitan area and of other communities."

The conference and walk were part of a life devoted to what, in her social scientist's language, Audrey calls "paradigmatic transformation," or, more simply, "training people in race relations."

8

A WOMAN CALLED ALICE

A Papua New Guinean teacher speaks the
truth to headhunters and to legislators.

AT A DINNER WELCOMING Queen Elizabeth to
Papua New Guinea in 1973, one of the queen's security guards
heard that a local guest, Alice Wedega, had visited Northern Ireland. "What on earth were you doing there?" he asked her.

In her direct fashion, Alice told the man that her great-grandfather had been a cannibal. "At that time," she said, "our people used
to kill and eat men. They would practice payback. That is, if one of
your side killed one of mine, my side would kill one of yours. But
the missionaries came from Europe to stop us doing all that. And
now I have been back to Northern Ireland to help the Europeans
there stop doing it." The guard, according to Alice, looked very
surprised. "So I told him how the good spirit had spoken in the
hearts of our people and taught them how to make enemies into
friends." In her attitude about the West, Alice shared the view of
another distinguished Papua New Guinean leader, Sir Paul Lapun:
"Maybe people going from here could give them something. For
all their progress and science and technology, they have forgotten

God. They have given us Christianity, medicine, education; this would be a chance for us to pay back."

Alice was the first female member of the Legislative Council of her country, the first Papuan guide commissioner, and the first woman to be decorated by the queen, becoming in 1982 Alice Wedega, Dame Commander of the Order of the British Empire. Dame Alice's reply to the security guard encapsulated both the extraordinary transition her country has worked through in one lifetime and the fulfillment of the words of missionary Charles Abel when he baptized her at the age of sixteen: "Someday God will send you to other parts of the world."

The effectiveness of Alice's work for peace in her own country and, later, in travels that took her not only to Ireland and other European countries but also to Ceylon (now Sri Lanka), India, and New Zealand stemmed from two solid foundations in her life. One was the influence of some unusual missionaries, and the other was a decision to turn her back on a hatred of white people, which, though understandable under the circumstances, might have soured her life for good. Plus she has an unshakable faith that the good spirit can speak to anyone.

She became what Sir John Guise, a former governor general of Papua New Guinea, called "a bright, shining beacon to a worried and frustrated world." In a foreword to her autobiography, *Listen, My Country*, he wrote, "I can think of no other woman leader who can equal the achievements and distinction that she has achieved for her beloved homeland."

Alice Wedega was born in 1905 in the village of Alo Alo in Milne Bay, on the eastern tip of what was then Papua. Her people had lived on the island of New Guinea for thousands of years before the white people came. Her father and other relations would tell her about seeing the first whites; they could not imagine who they might be or where they had come from.

At the age of eight, Alice was sent to help an aunt look after her children. The aunt lived at the mission station at Kwato, which was founded by Charles Abel in 1891. He was trained by the London Missionary Society and was farseeing and different from most European missionaries of his time. He saw the need to develop the practical as well as the spiritual lives of the villagers. Even in those days he looked forward to a time when Papua would be self-governing. Indeed, grandchildren of the first Papuans educated by him are now in public service in the independent nation.

There is a story told about Abel in the early days of the mission: Walking along a forest track one afternoon, he surprised a group of village women, who fled. One of the Papuans with him called out, "It's not a white man, it's only a missionary!" The women came back, apologizing to Abel with the words, "Oh, we thought you were a white man."

Kwato was a seventy-two-acre island, and supplies were brought once a month by ship from Australia. By the time Alice arrived, the mission was well established; it had the most advanced mission school in Papua with some thirty children, as well as a sawmill and boatbuilding works. The children were taught to read and write and learned how to work and to take responsibility. "We grumbled, but the discipline was good training for us," Alice recalled later. "Today, when I see many things done haphazardly I criticize, but I see now that often no one has taken the trouble to teach young people to do things properly, as we were taught at Kwato."

Religious training, Alice emphasized, was always an important part of their education: "Today children are clever but they sometimes have no manners or respect for God, or man. Our children in those days were not clever but they had discipline. Our parents disciplined us all the time. When we had too much fun we were punished."

Abel was concerned that the children's education should include developing a skill in some craft or industry so that on their return to the villages, the Papuans could put their knowledge to good use in building up the country. But his first aim was to train those at the mission to be Christians and to know that God was a God of love. Alice and others went out as young trainees to take what they had learned about Christianity to the villages in the area. They would travel between the islands in sixty-foot dugout canoes, hugging the coast—a big adventure for a teenager.

"It is very difficult to describe the influence of Kwato," said the chairman of the Australian Overseas Committee when he visited the island in 1920 and reported back to Australia. "One has to see it, live in it, to realize fully its power as a Christian mission and its enormous possibilities."

Alice wrote in 1981, "We, of course, didn't realize what an influence Kwato was in Papua until we heard from other people many years later that the standards of excellence had been taken by the people trained at Kwato to their homes. Even today in remote places in Papua New Guinea, no matter how simple the home, you will find that same care and quality of life if the mothers were trained at Kwato."

A small printing press was sent from England, along with an Englishman to help the islanders learn how to work it. He expected to stay for a year, but within four months he felt that he was no longer needed. Alice took the course in bookbinding and printing and became the first bookbinder on the island. In 1927, she helped print a translation of the Gospels in Suau, the local language.

At the end of that year, Alice was invited to join a family in Sydney, Australia, as a servant. It was the only way Papuans could go overseas. She soon felt, however, that she was being treated more like a slave than a servant. Food, consisting of leftovers from the family meal, was left for her on the veranda or in her room . At one point, the woman struck her, and Alice did not know where to turn for help. A hatred and bitterness began to build up in her. When the family took her with them to a home in the Blue Mountains, she could not enjoy the place because she had no rights. She had no bed of her own, having to wait until everyone went to sleep before she could use the couch in the living room. She had to wash in the chicken house and dig a hole for a toilet.

It was a happy day when her time in Australia was at an end and she could return to Kwato, free to tell people how she had been treated. "I warn you never to go to Australia with a European," she liked to say, "because that is the way they will treat you." She did not want Papuans to think that there were any good Australians.

In 1930, Charles Abel was killed in England in a road accident. Not sure what the future held, his son, Cecil, and sister, Phyllis, went with Alice and the others at the mission—brown and white— to a hill station called Duabo to spend a few days together to seek inspiration. Cecil spoke to them of a spiritual revival he and his brother had recently encountered in England. At its heart, he said, was the idea that in addition to praying to God people needed to take time to listen to him, that if people faced up to Christ's absolute standards of honesty, purity, unselfishness, and love, they could find out what God wanted them to do.

"When Cecil then told us about places in his own life where he had failed and been dishonest, it really got home to us. We felt more like a family than ever. We were no different from him, and we needed to look at our own lives, as he had done."

In the peace and quietness of that village, Alice and the others decided to see whether God would speak to them. They had a time of quiet together. "Jealousies, resentments and impurities that had been holding up the work of the mission for years came into the open and apologies were made," writes Alice. She herself thought back to the chicken house in Australia and all that she had said about it. "I saw how I had tried to make my people feel all white people were bad. I had to face my hatred of that Australian lady. I saw where I had failed in absolute love. I couldn't ask her forgiveness because she had since died, but I told my friends about my resentment against her and I asked God to forgive me. Freedom from this resentment opened up a whole new life for me." It was then that Alice decided, as she put it, to give up all her own plans, including marriage, and devote herself to serving her country.

She and the others returned to Kwato with a new unity and readiness to follow wherever the Holy Spirit would lead them. It was decided that those at Kwato would go out to the other villages and share their experiences of change. The first village they visited was Maivara, where Alice and the others described how they had learned to listen to the good spirit and how doing so had changed their lives. One of the chief rainmakers decided to follow their example and publicly destroyed the things he used for making magic. Other sorcerers went to the homes of people they had killed and asked for forgiveness.

"The new spirit began to spread like a fire," wrote Alice. "Women were no longer just the property of men, children were wanted and cared for. People lost their fear of each other as sorcery died out. They built new houses and cleaned their villages. Getting together for 'power house,' or times of prayer, listening and sharing experiences, became an important part of village life, and each morning a conch shell would be blown to remind everyone that it was time to get up, to bathe in the river, and to have a time of listening. It is astonishing, but we heard later that the change that came to this area began to solve problems that had worried the government for some years."

Then, courageously, the Kwato people moved out to the more remote villages of the headhunters. In some places, the jungle was so thick that during the day it was like a kind of permanent twilight. Witchcraft and sorcery held sway over the people, who lived in continual fear. Villages had been broken up because of the distrust. When asked why they would not trust one another and live together, the villagers replied, "If we live together we die." Since they did not know which of them was practicing witchcraft, they believed that if they kept apart they would be safe.

At the suggestion of the lieutenant governor, Sir Hubert Murray, Alice and her friends decided to see what they could do to end tribal fighting in the mountains halfway to the capital, Port Moresby. There, head-hunting was part of the traditional custom, and nobody seemed to be able to help people understand why they should stop. Alice and her friends went from village to village, spending a night or two in each. They had to ford rivers and climb mountains. When they arrived, people would often run away at first, thinking that they were the police. In every village, they gathered with the people to tell them about the good spirit and then pray with them.

This was a completely new experience for the villagers. When Alice and her friends prayed, all the villagers would look at them with their eyes open. Then one of the men would say, "Shut your eyes!" And, as Alice recalls with amusement, "If any woman kept her eyes open after that, she would be given a wallop. So the women obediently closed their eyes and held their babies' eyes shut as well." Sometimes nothing seemed to get through to the villagers except that these men and women were working with one another; they had come unarmed and without police protection, yet were unafraid.

As Alice and the others traveled, they learned why the disputes never seemed to come to an end. They saw the way hatred was kept alive from one generation to another. In some places, they discovered that young women were the cause of much of the killing, because a woman might not agree to marry a man until he had killed someone and brought the victim's finger to her to prove it.

"We did not try to teach these people," said Alice. "We let them find from the good spirit what he wanted them to know that day. In fact, *davalia*, finding, was the word that was used for listening to the spirit's directions. Soon every day people were finding things and telling all the others about it. It was amazing to see how fast the experience spread, how people learned to listen and to pray and to make friends with everyone. Sometimes a whole tribal group would ask forgiveness for the things they had done wrong." After one "peace feast," eighty-four men who had been headhunters sent a message to Cecil Abel about their change.

The lieutenant governor visited the area and discovered for himself that the killing had ended. He told Abel in 1937, "I don't know whether it is entirely your influence or not, but I can tell you that since you people have been there, I haven't had to try one single case."

On the invitation of Chief Belei, one of the headmen who had given up head-hunting, Alice returned to his village of Amau. "If there is to be any future for the Kunika [local tribe] people," he said, "we will have to change our ways or we will kill or be killed and our numbers will dwindle." A mission house and a school were constructed, where the children of the headhunters were soon being taught writing, reading, and arithmetic and given singing lessons. A hospital was built and, later, a church. Amau became a tidy village with well-built houses, flowering shrubs, and vegetable gardens. At the church, the broken spears of former warriors were hung on its walls, many of them notched from end to end, each notch representing a man who had been killed. Now the spears were a symbol that there would be no more fighting. Alice was to live in Amau for several years before and after World War II.

Some idea of the challenges Alice faced are described in *Doctor in Papua* by Berkeley Vaughan, who spent many years at Kwato:

She had to start from scratch with completely untrained children. Her pupils had long been accustomed to all sorts of depravity, and some of them showed the most vicious traits. They were cruel to animals and insects and were often even at each other's throats. The favorite game was murder: little toddlers would stalk, waylay, and finally do to death some hapless stray dog or cat. They seemed to exult in killing, and their parents had given encouragement to pugnacious impulses in the hope of breeding killers. Gradually these characteristics were eradicated, by the introduction of substitute games.

Alice set out to work to win these children as well as teach them. Instead of reproducing exactly the system and curriculum of existing schools in the very different circumstances of the Kwato district, she showed complete originality in her approach to the problem. Both she and her Papuan helpers felt that this school should be in keeping with the ideals and thinking of Kunika leaders, and with the new pattern of village life they were working out. If the children could relate their actions and decisions to the basic standards of Christ, they would be better equipped to carry further the new living that their parents were trying to establish. (p. 147)

The change in the parents during those years was so dramatic that Alice felt compelled to record their stories. When the Japanese invaded during World War II, she hid her interview notes in the jungle for safety: fortunately, they were later recovered. The simple, straightforward accounts of these men make moving reading as they tell of the people they murdered, how they did it, and how they spent years in jail. Then they tell of the revolutionary realization that they could win over their enemies instead of getting rid of them, and how they were able to survive under Japanese occupation.

As one of them, Biruma, told Alice: "Through my lies and false reports I brought five men to jail but I got off free. In that year the Kwato people came to our area, bringing the news about God. As I listened to all that they said, I felt deeply my sin in killing, lying, and bitterness of heart. The first thing God told me was, 'Stop killing your people. Make friends of your enemies and apologize for your long years of hatred and bitterness.' I started to think, 'How can I do that? Supposing I tell them about myself. *They* might kill *me*!' I was ashamed and frightened to do this, but God gave me the conviction and also the courage to make restitution for what I had done."

World War II was naturally a setback for the mission's work in developing the Milne Bay area. Its European staff had to be evacuated, and many of the local people had to go into hiding. The war years also prevented the introduction of new farming methods. But in 1945–46, Alice returned to show the local people how to improve their land and crops. While Mr. Cottrell-Dormer, the agricultural official who traveled with her, assembled the men, she gathered with the women. She soon realized that they needed help caring for sick children and instruction in hygiene and nutrition. She decided to set up a center where women could come for training and then return to their villages to teach others. With local help and without government assistance (which only came later), a training center was opened at Ahioma. Fifty young women attended that first year. The center soon became so well known that girls from all over Papua New Guinea were sent there.

It was from Ahioma that Alice went, in 1961, to the Legislative Council, becoming its first female member. This experience opened up a wider world and showed her where her people needed to take responsibility instead of being led by Australia. Her voice was sometimes an uncomfortable challenge in the chamber as she would always speak up and vote for what she felt the good spirit was telling her. "If a woman really thinks for her country, she will speak the truth and not have axes of her own to grind," was her conviction. She also represented her country at international conferences.

Alice had a deep conviction about the role of women in building unity between the tribes and different areas of her country and in speaking out "loudly and clearly [about] what we feel is right for the country." In the Legislative Council she set the pace; she voiced

Alice Wedega with girls from Milne Bay at the Cape Rodney market in 1976. Photograph by Alan Weeks.

her opinion on everything from the importation of films that she believed encouraged immorality and violence to the replacement of worthwhile food-producing businesses with breweries. To her, however, women's responsibility for home life was more important than anything else, even jobs: "Often we criticize our menfolk for using money on drink and other things and not caring about the home and children. The atmosphere our men feel in the home and the consideration they get from us will perhaps make them want to spend more time there."

Coming from a mission background, Alice's faith was always a dominant factor in her work for peace. But her own experience of freedom from hatred and the response of the Kunika people to the concept of the good voice were the bedrock of what she took in later years to the Sami people in northern Sweden, to villagers in western India, and to the Catholics and Protestants of Northern

Ireland. As Dr. Vaughan wrote, "If a primitive, deeply traditional people can alter their way of life so drastically, why should not a world divided by race, color, and religion find the same answer."

In a letter to the Port Moresby *Post-Courier* in October 1976, Alice described a recent visit to Amau where she had reminded the younger generation of what their parents had done in earlier days:

> First they built unity between the tribes. They built a church and broke their spears as a promise to stop their killing. This was done through God's guidance. Now the younger ones have drifted away from the vision their parents had in the past. Some of them live on their rubber plantations, thinking only of making money and buying trucks. But they and all their generation must build on the best of their parents' vision, for the sake of their own children, who have to carry on from the decisions we make. It is time to choose the best and never the second best, because in the future there will be much more difficult things happening they will have to know how to deal with.

Today the Abau-Amau area, where the headhunters lived, has a productive agricultural economy, growing rice and rubber and supplying vegetables to the capital.

Alice died on December 3, 1987, but the kind of training she received through the Kwato mission is still being passed on to young people in Milne Bay province by those that she trained. A grandson of Biruma is one of a group now building a new church. And a report from Milne Bay in 1993, written in Suau, describes an outreach to thirty-four villages in the region that is very much in the spirit of Alice's earlier adventures and a tribute to her pioneering work:

> Eleven of us set off, traveling from village to village on foot, in canoes and by truck. Up to two hundred people would gather in the evenings. We shared about listening to God. In some cases, husbands and wives decided to straighten their lives, build happy homes and return to the Church. Many

children came—at one village we counted 353. So we held meetings for them. After a time of listening they had no shyness in speaking of their dishonesty, or disobedience, to their parents, and apologized. *Rascals* [gang members] put things right with their community in public. Two *rascals* joined our team and were able to help other young men as they traveled. Once we had to swim a swollen river. One canoe capsized. Our guide was swept out to sea but was rescued. Crocodiles are plentiful in that area.

The eleven returned safe to Kwato for an Easter camp for a thousand people. They report that there is a constant flow of people there because "it is close to the Charles Abel Highway."

Alice rejoiced at her country's independence but was happy to see that the Australian flag was lowered with respect and reverence before the bird of paradise flag of Papua New Guinea was raised. She was pleased to see the emergence of her country and wanted it to set an example. "Papua New Guinea will never be a country without problems," she said, "but it could be known for the way we get over them."

9

OUR SAIDIE

*An Irish labor leader works for economic
justice and peace.*

"IF THE MEN WOULD pass more pubs and fewer resolutions, we'd be a good deal better off." This "Saidieism," as her sayings were known—a shot across the bows of some of her male trade union colleagues—is typical of the directness and the humor of one of Ireland's great women, Saidie Patterson. But her directness was coupled with a simplicity of faith that is reminiscent of her friend Mother Teresa. Indeed, Mother Teresa once said of Saidie, in what must be one of the more unusual tributes to a trade union leader and peacemaker, that she had kept her vows of poverty, chastity, and obedience as irrevocably as any nun. Betty Williams, the Belfast woman who, with Mairead Corrigan, received the 1976 Nobel Peace Prize, was asked on television if she knew Saidie. "You mean 'Our Saidie'?" she responded. Saidie Patterson was regarded as the mother of the peace movement in Northern Ireland.

The collapse of the cold war, the extraordinary Middle East handshakes, the emergence of a black-led government in South Africa, the breaking of the logjam on issues that for years seemed insuperable, have naturally raised the question: "And why not

Ireland?" Often held up as an example of an intractable problem, often used as a reproach to Christians because it is a Christian land with Christians killing one another, Ireland's own initiatives for peace are not always widely known, particularly the heroic quality of many of its women, of whom Saidie was a prime example. Saidie's life was perhaps a glimpse of the bridge building that must accompany any eventual political settlement. David Bleakley, a former Northern Ireland cabinet minister and author of *Saidie Patterson, Irish Peacemaker*, said at her funeral, "An Ireland full of Saidies would be an island at peace."

One day Saidie, a Protestant, was riding up the Shankill Road, in the Protestant heart of Belfast, on a bus. In front of her, two women started up about the sins of "them 'uns," the Catholics, egging each other on. Finally, Saidie could stand it no longer. She poked them with her umbrella and started in on them: "It's no use blaming, we're all part of what's wrong, it's we who need to start." Soon she was in full flow. The bus driver was so fascinated that he would not stop the bus to let anyone off in case they missed what she was saying. He took them all to the bus terminus, then turned around and said, "Now, I'll take you all home free."

Any profile of Saidie Patterson must draw liberally on her own words, her speeches and writings that reflected her life's commitment so well. Saidie was born in a working-class home off the Shankill Road in Belfast in 1906: "There was nothing fancy about how we or our neighbors lived. But we were proud of our homes and kept them spic and span. We hadn't a lot of furniture and the like, but we got the best we could and never ran into debt. And they were happy homes—not a lot in the way of this world's goods, but we shared what we had and everyone felt they belonged."

She lived in the same house all her life, proud of the fact that she never jumped out of the bowl that she was baked in: "Long-distance leadership is ultimately ineffective. If I started to live away from my people I'd no longer be one of them. I'd lose the things we share together; before long I would become a mere observer, writing and talking about them."

Saidie's father, William Patterson, was a blacksmith in the local shipyard who died when she was six: "A good Christian who loved his Methodist church and who read the Bible from cover to cover." Her mother was one of the poorly paid outworkers in the textile industry. When food was short—as it often was—like many women of the time, she chose to go without. Throughout her life, Saidie was always conscious of her mother's oft-repeated words at the family prayer circle: "If you see something wrong in this world and do nothing about it, you are committing a crime against the whole of humanity."

Saidie was twelve when her mother died in childbirth because the family could not afford the three shillings and six pence for a doctor: "As I stood in my dear mother's blood, I didn't shed a tear, but I felt a cross being put on my back and, at the same time, I felt a strange warmth coming into the room. Looking back now I am convinced it was the Holy Spirit. From that day on I put my hand to doing what I could for what was right, and the good Lord has honored the bargain that was made at my mother's bedside. That night I became an adult."

Saidie was left to look after baby Jean, who was three days old; her step-father, who became an invalid as a result of the shock of his wife's death, and six brothers and sisters. One brother had to emigrate because he could not get work in Ireland and was denied assistance from the state. Saidie became the breadwinner, going to work at Ewarts, one of the biggest local linen mills.

Years later, receiving an honorary degree from Britain's Open University, she said that her primary degree was obtained in the university of life; her university halls were the streets of Shankill and the Falls Road, and her teachers were the wise men and women reared in working-class homes. She reminded her audience what life was like early in the century, when textiles was one of the main industries and employed 100,000 workers, most of them women: "We were plentiful and cheap. The working week was one of fifty-five hours and many a time we worked sixty; and no overtime was paid. As for paid holidays, they were unheard of. In those days our women worked to six o'clock at night; babies were often born the same evening, perhaps two hours later. And the same women were back on the job in forty-eight hours, hardly fit to stand all day on the job. It was either that or lose the job and the desperately needed money that went with it. We who produced the finest table linen in the world had to be content with the newspapers on our tables, too poor to buy what we produced. Often we slept on sheets made from flour bags."

The only time that Saidie is known to have departed from her lifelong principle of nonviolence involved one such young woman who had just had a baby. It happened in the early days of her involvement with the women textile workers, and it nearly cost her her job. To assist the young mother, she and others had made her a stool. The foreman came around and was furious at seeing the woman sitting down. He gave her a severe shaking and she collapsed, her unraveled hair running the risk of getting caught in the machines and scalping her. At that moment, Saidie forgot her pacifist and Methodist upbringing and rushed at the foreman, slashing his face with her scissors. "By the time I had finished, his face looked like the Stars and Stripes of America."

Saidie was summoned to the manager's office and was told that unless she apologized immediately and guaranteed good behavior in the future, she would be fired and blacklisted in the industry. She went home to talk with her family. Her invalid stepfather said, "Daughter, your mother would not want you to apologize for something you were right to do. Go back and take your stand, and the Lord will look after you."

When she was first called to the manager's office, the women in the factory had hammered their scissors on their looms to show their solidarity. As she returned to give her answer, she asked them to stop their machines: "We will let the bosses hear your support in a silent factory." Threatened again with the loss of her job, she told the manager, "Well, sir, what you have just done will make a good story for the *Belfast Telegraph* tonight. My girls and I are going to march down now to give the facts to them. I wonder how it will look in print to your customers when they see, 'Ewarts sack weaver for defending young mother from assault.'"

Saidie kept her job, and for twenty years she worked to improve conditions and to get women into the trade union movement. She also became one of the best weavers in the country. In those days, trade union solidarity was for men only, and employers tended to keep men happy at the expense of women. She inspired women to become shop stewards, to canvass for new members, and to collect union dues even though to do so often carried the risk of dismissal. She helped the men widen their concerns. With the backing of Ernest Bevin of the Transport and General Workers' Union (later Britain's Labour foreign secretary), she became the first female official in the union and started unionizing Ewarts. "The job I am offering you will be as big as a mountain," Bevin told her, "and I can only promise you a spoon to dig it." Saidie's response was, "It's amazing what a woman can do with a spoon."

A crucial moment came in 1940, with the demand for full trade union membership among linen workers. Saidie led a seven-week strike, which drew nationwide attention. Over a million leaflets were distributed, and although the strike did not achieve its immediate objective, partly because it was wartime, it catapulted Saidie to national prominence. It also established the framework for new industrial relations, and led to a transformation in working conditions, earnings, and welfare. By the end of that year, there was a 15 percent increase in wages and an agreement for holidays with pay. It had been a clear demonstration of the power of the women.

Saidie's new prominence brought her into increasingly close touch with the leaders of the Labour party, through which she worked for social welfare, organized huge public rallies, and was an effective money raiser. In 1956, she became the first woman chairperson of the Northern Ireland Labour party.

In the late 1940s, a new dimension had come into her life. Just as her friend Alice Wedega (see Chapter 8) of Papua New Guinea had been liberated by finding an answer to her hatred of white Australians, Saidie found wider effectiveness through an answer to her bitterness toward employers, particularly the "linen lords." She found it at the first Caux conference in 1946, where, she said, she joined "a band of comrades from every walk of life and every land and every continent who've surrendered their lives to God and who live their lives under the guidance of the Holy Spirit." It led her to regard the whole world as her parish—as one of her heroes,

John Wesley, had. And nearly thirty years later, in 1975, she was recognized by the Women's International League for Peace and Freedom as one of the fifty most prestigious women in the world.

Saidie never forgot the words of a challenge that was given to her during her first visit to Caux: "Suppose you were given all the weapons you needed, and suppose all your hard men were destroyed and gone—where would you go from there? Do you really believe that class hatred is the answer—when you're filled with it, where does it get you?"

The first steps were not easy. One of the hardest decisions she made on her return to Ireland was to apologize to an employer, even though she felt that he was 99 percent to blame for their disagreement. After three days of turmoil, she apologized for her "1 percent" and a new era began in her life. "Still an unequaled champion and honored by her union for her work," writes Bleakley, "she insisted that labor and management must find ways to cooperate across the class divide."

She was criticized. Not everyone responded to her idea of bridge building: "I don't want to give the impression that all went smoothly from then on. That's not the way of life. And I certainly don't want to give the impression that all my trade union friends and the industrialists agreed with me. They did not. Some secretly and others openly opposed me. But none of them managed to produce a superior idea able to replace the strife that was harming all of us."

Earlier, she had not been held back by antiquated attitudes on the factory floor. Now, she was not going to be hampered by those who still wanted to pit class against class or, as she got more involved in the sectarian problems of her country, by those who wanted to hang on to their prejudices toward the other group. As she said, "A moral revolution is no place for timid people."

After her retirement from union work, Saidie began to get more involved in the major division in her country, that between Protestants and Catholics. Again she used her straightforward approach: "There's no such thing as 'orange' and 'green' tears; we all weep together. We must decide which we prefer, to bury the hatchet or bury the dead."

She told the British Labour party conference in Blackpool in 1962: "Ireland has become a model of division. People come from all over the world to see how we do it. Yet there is no country in Europe which has had to fight for bread and work as much as Ireland. If we spent as much time struggling for one another as we do in fighting over the past, what a people we would be, what an inspiration we could become to struggling humanity."

Saidie became chair of the Women Together movement, which was founded after a cleaner in the Belfast Gas Works had a persistent dream that the women of Northern Ireland were uniting to tell the violent ones: "Put away your guns and your bombs. Give us back peace." Their message was simple, said Saidie: "If you face a wall of hate, climb it with help in your hands and hope in your heart." She illustrates how they worked: "Our streets were in a mess. A Roman Catholic road sweeper would be afraid to go into a Protestant area or a Protestant into a Roman Catholic area. We felt a dirty street was a beaten street, so we persuaded our neighbors to sweep with us. Diehards on both sides were suspicious. They asked, 'Who gave you permission to sweep?' We replied that those were our streets. We edged closer to the battlefield. As rioters traded bricks and petrol bombs with rubber bullets of the army, we linked arms and spanned the streets, holding our ground against missiles and jeers. Mothers advanced arm in arm, scattering the youngsters home; soldiers watched in wonder at a weapon more powerful than any they carried."

As chair of Women Together, Saidie led a march of fifty thousand women through the Protestant and Catholic areas of the city, which she regarded as the crowning experience of her life. She said on that occasion: "The last time I walked up the Shankill Road with Catholics was in the early 1930s when we were marching to the workhouse for bread and some of us were in bare feet. Today we walk up the Shankill not as Protestants or Catholics but as children of the King of Kings."

For her work in bringing Catholics and Protestants together, Saidie was given awards, but she was also attacked. During one rally, when she was already in her seventies, she was beaten up, but some Catholic women saved her. She was in the hospital for months with an injured spine, but all the time she was enlisting, as she put it, converts for the cause. "Isn't it amazing," she observed, "how Protestants and Catholics share one another's blood on the transfusion table." She wrote from the hospital: "My daily experience is that the Holy Spirit is uniting humanity through men and women who listen and obey. I believe Ireland will be used to take God's answer to the world."

Even in her late seventies, crippled with arthritis and hampered by her injuries, she would be out touring the countryside, attending four or five meetings a week. She particularly loved to talk to young people. "I'm all right from the neck up," she would joke.

Saidie felt that brickbats and bouquets had one thing in common: they got in the way of the work to be done. "Anyway, why should we worry whether our work is noticed or not? It will be recorded in the final reckoning that really counts."

When Saidie was given the first World Methodist Peace Award, the citation stated: "She has sat with the men of violence and dissuaded them from bombing and shooting." It was given "for her courageous work, her creativity in crossing hostile barriers to mediate between persons on both sides and her long-term efforts for the cause of peace." At the very moment that the cameras were filming her reaction to the award, word came that her great-nephew had been shot an hour earlier in an Irish Republican Army (IRA) ambush. "The news made my blood run cold," she said, "but I prayed that bitterness would not enter my heart. I was more determined than ever to continue the work for peace."

Later that night she said on television: "Young man, you who killed someone dear to me today have done a terrible thing. But there is no bitterness, only sadness in my heart. Nor do I want anyone in Northern Ireland to react with bitterness. We have enough of that; these things are not in our hands. Robert was a good boy who loved his country and tried to serve it well. He is with his God tonight. Someday you who have done the killing will have to meet your Maker to explain your action. In the meantime, we who believe in peace will see that the work goes on without bitterness in our hearts."

The *Yorkshire Post* (September 14, 1977) quoted her: "What keeps me going is the fact that more and more of our women, both

Roman Catholic and Protestant, are telling the men that it is better to sit around a table and talk than stand around a graveyard and cry. Those tears are not colored in orange and green. They are tears of sorrow. I never believe in judging a man by the church he attends on Sunday or the color of his skin, but by his character. It is not being a Roman Catholic or a Protestant which will create peace. It is being a Christian. Peace is not going to be achieved either by the politicians or the army. It is going to be done by personal contact. That is what I believe in."

When the Pope visited Ireland in 1979, Saidie was one of those who helped collect half a million Protestant signatures urging him to visit the north. When she took the signatures to the papal nuncio, he invited her to speak at the International Vigil for Peace and Reconciliation to be held in the pope's honor in Dublin's St. Patrick's Cathedral. She said at the vigil, "Which one of you here tonight picked your parents? Why then do we battle about our origins?" Describing the occasion later, she said, "I had a long talk with the good Lord. He told me what to say. I started by asking if everybody there that night were arrested for being a Christian would there be enough evidence to convict you and me. I told them it was one thing to pray during a crisis, but it is another thing to live so that it does not happen again." She received eight hundred letters after her address.

Looking back on the changes that had occurred in her lifetime, Saidie was pleased. When the queen of England decorated Saidie in 1953, she asked her how it was going with the women. Saidie replied, "Well, ma'am, once our women were just pairs of hands. Now, ma'am, they are royal souls like yourself." But Saidie was also very conscious of new challenges: "A bloodless revolution has taken place. Gone are the days of crude hiring and firing, with all its indignity. There is the change in personal living standards. We can now choose our food and so many have more than enough to eat. The changes in working conditions—canteens, first-aid rooms, showers, and the like. In welfare benefits, pension, sickness and unemployment rates, the strides taken have been enormous. But there's still much missing in today's world. We have made great material advances and must welcome them and the opportunities

Saidie Patterson plants a memorial Peace Cross for her great-nephew in Belfast in 1979. Photograph from the Bleakley Collection.

they bring. But we must use these opportunities to set our people really free. How do we deal with a situation when purses are full but hearts are empty—weakened family life, neglect of children; many on tranquilizers, others on drink, some using guns. Add to all this the plight of the lonely and aged people, and the bigotry and violence which divide our people. Move forward to the land of all our dreams; a land in which ignorance, fear, and hate shall give place to liberty, justice, and peace."

In 1975, she gave a statement for International Women's Year: "Mass poverty, hunger, war, racial conflict cry out for a solution. Man can fly through space, walk on the moon, calculate with computers, and transplant hearts, yet seldom has he felt more trapped by processes he cannot control. 'The hand that rocks the cradle rules the world' may be true, but we must help women to play their part in building a better world, starting with themselves and their own country. Throughout my life I have had direct contact with about ninety thousand women, and the first thing I had to do was to help them see that they counted, as they do, and had much to contribute to society. We all want peace, but we have not yet paid the price for peace—the price of facing, with God's help, where we and our nation have been wrong."

In a statement a year later that was broadcast on the Women's World Day of Prayer, she said: "In order to tackle our problems we must not be hooked on power or hate. The power of God can break the power of hate in our lives. We are all free to choose what we want to live for and what we want to give. We women can do what the politicians have failed to do. We are the givers of life and we can bring our country back from the hell of recent years. Today the disease is hate. Instead of taking the burden of the whole country on our shoulders, we can begin to work for the ideal by seeking reconciliation with those who are near to us. Instead of always asking what the government can do to bring about peace, or even what the church can do, if we were to ask what 'I' can do, and proceed, in however small a way, to generate peace and reconciliation in our society, then progress can be made wherever we live."

Summing up her life on the BBC, the Rev. Gordon Grey said, "In her own life she wove together in an exquisite pattern the sometimes severed strands of justice and of peace, of warm evangelical faith and wide ecumenical vision, of spiritual depth and social concern, of fearlessness and compassion."

Asked once how she would like to be remembered, Saidie referred to the tribute given by Victor Halley, one of Ireland's respected trade union figures, on behalf of her friends in the Irish Labour movement and beyond. He wrote: "If faith can move mountains, then that is the sort of faith Saidie possesses and with which she is possessed. She articulated in language that was understandable and free from jargon the feelings of women workers in textiles. Her weapons were truth and justice. Nor was her effort a purely local one. For, if John Wesley traveled the length and breadth of England on horseback, Saidie spanned the world on a thousand horse power."

David Bleakley, who spoke at Saidie's funeral on January 19, 1985, in the Shankill Road Methodist church where she had worshiped all her life, said that he had once said to Mother Teresa, "Mother, you remind me of Saidie Patterson."

Mother Teresa replied, "I may remind you of Saidie Patterson but there's a vital difference. Saidie Patterson has moved into service without really knowing it. She has taken the vows of chastity, poverty, and obedience. I go home at night to the love of my sisters, and if I take ill at night, they will be there to care for me and to tend for me. Saidie Patterson goes home at night on her crutches to Woodvale Street to a tiny house, and she has no one there but her Lord and Maker to turn to in her darkest hours. That's a special kind of dedication."

Bleakley reassured the mourning congregation that in her last weeks, Saidie had lost none of her faith or her sparkle. "I said to her, 'Saidie, it looks like you're going.' She replied, 'David, don't worry. I'm taking an earlier bus than you are.'"

10

A YEN TO SERVE

*A Japanese woman widens her country's
responsibility to Asia.*

THE SIXTY-FOUR JAPANESE—the largest delegation
to leave their country since World War II—were amazed as their
bus rolled to a stop in front of Mountain House in Caux. They
were amazed not only at the hundreds of people from all over the
world who had gathered outside to welcome them to the 1950
international conference but also at the fact that the Japanese flag
was flying. It was a moving moment, Sen Nishiyama recalled at a
1993 diplomatic party. Back home, under the American occupation, flying the flag was still forbidden. It was part of that welcome
back into the family of nations that caused French Foreign Minister Robert Schuman to say at the 1951 signing of the Japanese peace
treaty in San Francisco that the people of Caux had made peace
with Japan two years before the political leaders signed it.

Along with the political figures in that 1950 delegation—the
governors, the leaders of industry and the trade unions, and the
mayors of Hiroshima and Nagasaki—were ten women. One of
them was quiet, self-effacing Yukika Sohma, who was then serving
largely as an interpreter. Indeed, she and Sen Nishiyama, who

worked with the U.S. embassy, pioneered on this trip to the West what had previously been thought impossible—simultaneously interpreting from and to Japanese. As the Japanese traveled around Europe and America, Yukika and Sen were their voice to the world. And it was an unusual voice.

Long before the Japanese prime minister's 1993 apologies to neighboring countries for Japan's wartime actions, even before the apologies by Niro Hoshijima (interpreted by Yukika Sohma) and Shidzue Kato referred to in Chapter 6, these sixty-four men and women had faced up to past wrongs. Two parliamentary members of the delegation were invited to speak on the floors of the U.S. Senate and House of Representatives. Their apologies to the law-makers caused the *New York Times* (July 19, 1950) to write, "For a moment we could see out of the present darkness when all men may become brothers." The *Saturday Evening Post* (July 29, 1950) stated, "Perhaps even Americans could think up a few past occa-sions of which it could be safely admitted, 'We certainly fouled things up that time.'"

The delegation's return to Japan produced dramatic results, as attested to in Basil Entwistle's book *Japan's Decisive Decade*. But only in more recent years have the remarkable contributions of Yukika Sohma found expression—contributions that have led to her being decorated by the governments of Japan and Korea and to a change in traditional Japanese attitudes. In a long and productive career, she has never held public office, but she has also never waited for the politicians to act when she felt that something needed to happen. And sometimes they have followed her lead.

Yukika is some fifteen years younger than her friend Shidzue Kato, but she has had to fight many of the same battles for women's emancipation. She was blessed with remarkable parents, from whom she draws much inspiration.

Her father, Yukio Ozaki, is revered as the father of Japanese parliamentary democracy. He set a world record in parliamentary participation, serving sixty-three years in the Diet, returning for twenty-five consecutive terms. He was also the mayor of Tokyo for nine years, during which time he presented Washington, D.C., with its cherry trees as a gesture of gratitude to Theodore Roosevelt, who had initiated the peace talks that ended the Russo-Japanese War. He spent a lifetime opposing war, even when it was politically and personally dangerous to do so. In 1921, for instance, he attacked the government for allocating half the national revenue for armaments. Increasing Japanese arms, he argued, would only invite an adversary to do likewise; national security would be threatened, not assured. He always put conscience before party loyalty and would not allow his conscience to be compromised or his mouth sealed by ennoblement. The first edition of the Japanese *Reader's Digest* contains an article by Yukika about her father.

Yukika's mother was the daughter of a Baron Ozaki (no relation to Yukika's father). As a young man, he had been selected by the Meiji government to study in England and had married Bathia Catherine, the daughter of his tutor, William Morrison. Morrison was a man of letters who had also tutored many of the other Japanese who were to rise to prominence. According to Mary Fraser, the wife of a British minister to Japan, Catherine was, "a charming and intelligent woman, but she was English to the backbone, and it was impossible for her to appreciate or sympathize with anything that was not British." So it was not surprising that after five years she and Baron Ozaki separated by mutual consent.

When she was sixteen, Yukika's mother, Yei Theodora Ozaki, came to live with her father in Japan. By her father's decree, she was henceforth to be "only Japanese," though she never learned to speak Japanese well. She became a teacher and a writer, first taking up her pen to dispel misconceptions of Japanese women that existed in Western minds. "When I was last in England and Europe and found by the questions asked that very mistaken notions about Japan, and especially about its women, existed generally," she said, "I determined if possible to write so as to dispel these wrong conceptions. Hence my stories of Japanese heroines."

In 1904, Yei got to know Yukio Ozaki, already the mayor of Tokyo, through the mistakes of a mailman who, owing to the similarity of the surname, often got confused and delivered her mail to the mayor's office. "From the moment when the two first met, at a big dinner party, and laughed together over the postman's mistakes," wrote Mary Fraser, "the result was a foregone conclusion."

Yei wrote some time later, describing her life in Tokyo society: "One night I may dine at a state banquet with cabinet ministers and foreign ambassadors, or with distinguished visitors like Mr. and Mrs. Taft, who recently visited this country; the next will find me with a purely Japanese party at the Maple Club. I assist at the court functions, the imperial wedding receptions; I act as sponsor or go-between at Japanese marriage ceremonies; I see all the ins and outs of Japanese life. I seem to live in the heart of two distinct civilizations, those of the East and the West, but the East is my spirit's fatherland. My mind still turns for companionship to the great ones of the past, the heroines of my country's history. I find greater pleasure in the old classical drama of the 'No,' with its Buddhist teachings and ideals, its human tragedies of chivalry and of sorrow, than in all the sensational and spectacular modern drama. But my greatest happiness is my home life, in the companionship of my baby daughter, in the few short hours that my husband can snatch from his work to devote to me."

Yei used to tell her daughter, Yukika, "It is said, 'East is East and West is West and never the twain shall meet,' but they are met in you!" International and interracial marriages were uncommon in those days, and Yukika had to make up her mind early on to which culture she belonged. She also had to make up her mind whether her father was right in his outspoken political beliefs, particularly about disarmament, or whether he was, as many diehards portrayed him, a traitor to his country.

He often received physical threats. "On one occasion," Yukika recalls, "two truckloads of ruffians stormed into our house shouting that they had come to take his life. Father and I escaped from the back of the house, climbed over the wooden fence of the factory next door, and took refuge in its boiler room. We had planned to go on a two-day trek on horseback, and we went ahead with this plan, escorted by policemen on bicycles. I was nervous, but my father said jokingly, 'This is the road along which criminals were escorted during the feudal days. It's a rare occasion to be treated like this, so let's enjoy as much as we can.'"

From an early age, Yukika was a rebel herself. Before she was in her teens, she clashed with a nun at a Catholic convent because she dared to ask in chapel why you were allowed to kill in a war when one of the Ten Commandments was that thou shalt not kill. She was told to leave the chapel, and she never returned. At the Peeresses' School, there was a Korean princess in her class. Yukika asked her, "If I were in your place I would be working for the independence of my country, why aren't you?" Her teacher told her firmly not to say such things. When the teacher asked the class what they were all planning for the future, Yukika was the only one who said that she was going to work—something unusual for a girl from her background. The teacher summoned her to her office. "Don't you ever disgrace the school by acting foolishly," she was told.

At the age of fourteen, Yukika insisted on being allowed to sit in the gallery of Parliament. Her ambition was to attend the university and go into politics. Neither avenue was open to women at the time, however, and when she was told that the constitution did not allow women to serve in Parliament, she said that she would have to change the constitution. But since changing the constitution was a little beyond her, Yukika decided that she would work to better the plight of women. Her friends were skeptical of her ability to help because she did not know what Japanese family life was really like. "It was then I decided to marry into a Japanese family in order to be able to do something for Japanese womanhood."

In August 1931, Yukika accompanied her father to the United States, where he had been invited by the Carnegie Foundation for International Peace and where her mother was undergoing medical treatment for sarcoma. Yukika and her father went on to England, where she attended an English finishing school—the Monkey Club—passed the exam to enter the London School of Economics, and was "enchanted with the labor movement." They were joined in May by her mother, but Yei's condition worsened, and in December she died. In February, Yukika returned with her father to Japan.

In the 1930s, Yukika was very much ahead of her times. Dressed in riding pants, she would gun her motorcycle through the Tokyo streets. This was an era when, as she says, Japanese women were meant "to look like dolls." One day a young man, Yasu Sohma, admired her bike, and she gave him a ride on the seat behind her.

Two days later he asked her for a date. She was surprised when he rode up on the most expensive motorcycle to be had. In 1937, Yasu, a viscount from a generations-old family with feudal estates in central Japan, became her husband. "The marriage was the talk of the town," she says, "because it had not been arranged; a love marriage was a faux pas to aristocrats, because I was the daughter of a man in politics, and because of my mixed blood, which was the last straw. It speaks for Yasu's independent mind and courage to follow his own ideas rather than to succumb to pressure."

The years leading to the outbreak of World War II were, Yukika says, "like living in suffocation." One after another, laws were passed to crush liberal thinking. "It was as if some power unknown to us was gradually engulfing the nation, and rational thinking was being replaced by chauvinist outcry. One longed for fresh air."

The bright spot for her at this time was that she began to face up to many of the fears in her life by taking time for quiet reflection to come to grips with them. She realized that although passionate about peace in the world, she sometimes contributed to war at home. She apologized to her mother-in-law and to her grandmother-in-law for saying one thing and thinking another. Her husband, observing the difference in her, asked, "Are you all right? Maybe you should go see a doctor." Perhaps it was this experience that enabled her to tell an Australian conference many years later, "I have committed myself to opening up the horizon of our women, not just 'liberation' but liberating ourselves from the self-will that hardens inside so that we can play our rightful role as women."

During World War II, Yasu was conscripted and sent to Manchuria, where Yukika joined him for two years. After the war when they traveled to Europe—which she thought of as going "home" to England—she was shocked to discover the depth of the anti-Japanese sentiment she encountered. Like most Japanese, she had been sheltered from the full extent of Japanese atrocities and the world's reaction to them. She made an effort to find out exactly what had gone on, and although she had always been personally opposed to Japanese militaristic policies, wherever she went in Europe she boldly stood up and apologized for what her nation had done.

She became involved internationally, interpreting and representing her country, eventually becoming president of the Federation of Asian Women's Associations, an organization of which she is still honorary vice president. In 1950, she accompanied her father to the United States at the invitation of the American Council on Japan. Thanks to the initiative of two former U.S. Ambassadors to Japan, William R. Castle and Joseph C. Grew, Ozaki was presented to both houses of Congress and spoke at forums contributing to a better understanding between the countries. His hosts' purpose was to prepare the American public for the coming peace treaty, and Ozaki was selected because of his clean record in opposing the war.

Ozaki died in 1954. The previous year, he had been made an honorary member of the Diet and an honorary citizen of Tokyo. In 1960, the Ozaki Memorial Hall and Clock Tower were built in his memory. Yukika is vice-chairperson of the Ozaki Yukio Memorial Foundation. She has also served on various government commissions, becoming a member of Japan's sixty-member National Advisory Board, and is president of the Japan-Korea Women's Friendship Association.

At the end of 1978, Yukika received a letter from a friend in Canada; enclosed was a report on Asia that called Japan a shameful nation because of its refusal to take in Southeast Asian refugees. It stated that the word *humanitarian* had no place in the Japanese lexicon, that the country thought only in economic terms.

When Yukika talked with government officials about Japan's image overseas and, in particular, its reluctance to help with the refugee problem, she got nowhere. A Foreign Ministry official told her, "There is no reason for us to pay attention to the meddlesome words of others." When she approached a senior member of the Diet, he said, "It's no good. You won't get anywhere with this. We have a large population, we are a single people, and we simply cannot admit that sort of people."

She began to talk publicly about the need for Japan to change its policy. "In Japan," she says, "we had become so selfish that we were not thinking of the suffering of these people." She enlisted Minao Masumoto, who was with the Liberal Democratic party, to work with her. She also talked with Mrs. Ohira, whose husband was then prime minister. She prevailed on a friend, Renzo

Yanigasawa, a Democratic Socialist senator, to raise the matter in a Diet committee. When he did so, the cabinet minister in charge answered, "We'll see something is done." In April, the cabinet decided to take in five hundred refugees.

Yukika recruited a group of mostly university leaders to help with the refugee problem. Among them was Professor Masunori Hiratsuka, who had written in an article that in the UN Year of the Youth, he wanted to see Japanese young people develop hearts that cared for others. He drew in the heads of private schools and colleges. Mrs. Miki, the wife of a future prime minister, joined the campaign. Many who knew Yukika's father responded as well.

Yukika told the press that she wanted to help the refugees *and* the Japanese. If Japan kept closing its heart, the country would become isolated from the rest of the world, which would be disastrous. Japan needed to learn to care for others. Money was needed not only from businesses but from ordinary people. Asked on television what her plans were, Yukika said, "If every Japanese gives one yen, we will have at least 120 million yen." She also said that she needed an office. That same day, an office was provided by Makoto Yanase, the chairman of an international volunteer organization, and soon money was pouring in.

The local post office had to put on extra staff to deal with the over twenty thousand letters Yukika received, which were often accompanied by moving comments. For instance, children wrote that they were giving up candy or were walking to save money; a husband and wife who were both seriously ill wrote, "We used to think we were unfortunate, but we realize now that the Cambodians are far worse off"; the father of a family of six who had finally saved enough to buy himself a suit wrote, "I guess the suit can wait"; a Christian family decided to send the money they would have used for Christmas gifts.

A host of volunteers joined her. Many had been looking for an avenue to do this sort of work; others had already been doing it elsewhere. Tadamasa Fukiura, for example, had been in Bangladesh with the Japan Overseas Cooperation Volunteers, the Japanese Peace Corps. In November 1979, Yukika founded the Association to Aid Indochinese refugees, the first private refugee relief organization in Japan. There were fifty founding members, and Yanase's daughter, Fusako Tozawa, became its secretary-general. "The initiative opened the way for ordinary people to actually do something concrete," she says.

Within three months, Yukika had reached her financial target. The *Japan Times* headlined her words: "I found a gold mine in the hearts of the Japanese people." "There are many individuals who want to care," she says, "and I have been learning to tap the resources that are hidden in each."

Speaking in Caux in 1980 about her reasons for initiating the aid program, she said, "I was ashamed that my government was doing so little for the Indochinese refugees. In Japan we are not trained to do so. Our bureaucrats are so efficient. When they get going they do the job without asking the people's help. So people don't know what to do. Also the concept of social welfare and voluntary service is relatively new in a society where the welfare of each family member is the responsibility of the head of the family. Today, refugees from Indochina are jolting the Japanese out of three decades of self-centered complacency and forcing us to open our hearts to our Asian neighbors. When we Japanese open our purses, it is a sign that we have opened our hearts. I want to keep Japan's heart open so that my country will not be a menace, as she once was, but an asset to the world."

Unless she kept reminding them, Yukika believed that people would "sleep on what they have done and then forget." She expanded the work of her association to other parts of Asia and to Africa, changing the name to the Association to Aid Refugees. "Just as we need to think for other families and not just our own, so we have to care for other nations. In fact, we may find that the real interests of our country are best served by being unselfish and caring," she says.

She discovered that Cambodian refugees needed housing because their huts had been burnt down. She found that bamboo huts could be built for twenty thousand yen each (less than one hundred dollars), so she launched a second appeal with the theme: "Don't you want a second house—in Cambodia? You won't be living there, but we'll put your name on it." Again the public

Yukika Sohma in 1984 at a Cambodian refugee camp in an area named Tokyo Village after the Japanese who donated money to build two hundred houses there. Photograph by Yukihisa Fujita.

responded generously. Then, when there was a cold wave in Southeast Asia, she asked for a thousand tons of clothing for a million refugees in Thailand and elsewhere. She gave a time limit of two weeks and enlisted two transport companies with eighty thousand agents all over the country. The company presidents put up posters announcing that any package addressed to the refugees would be transported at half price. The target was exceeded. She also received more than thirty million yen for shipping costs, and she went to Thailand to deliver the first thousand tons in person. From there she moved on to helping Afghani refugees. Her constant theme is that there is a battle between right and wrong in our hearts—a choice we have to make daily.

Her association has two thousand members who give regularly, with many others contributing as new projects are presented. They have started giving scholarship aid to those seeking higher education, and by the end of 1993, they had helped more than a thousand young people. In 1993, they sent 130,000 handmade bags containing gifts of pencils and other items to schoolchildren in Cambodia from the children of Japan. They opened a center for disabled people in Phnom Penh that provides vocational training and repairs wheelchairs, and in 1993, they donated one hundred wheelchairs for adults and thirty for children. They also started Support 21, a legal body under the jurisdiction of the Welfare Ministry, to help foreigners living in Japan who are in need.

For the past ten years, popular singers have given an annual concert to raise money. It is called Jagaimo Kai (potato association) because some two hundred years earlier, the potato was introduced from Java and played a role in alleviating famine. This musical group started in 1984 to help in Africa and collected thirty million yen in one evening. Five volunteer workers are in Zambia helping with vocational training and medical assistance. Books for a library and some scholarships have also been given, and a hundred tons of rice were sent in toasted powder form to Somalia. Indeed, whenever there is an earthquake or other natural disaster, the organization—thanks to efficient workers—can respond swiftly.

Yukika credits her success to the others who help. "I am often tempted to feel that I can do things myself," she says. "I have accepted that I cannot do anything worthwhile in my own strength. All I need to do is to be prepared for God to use me. Japan, too, tends to think she can do things on her own but needs to learn to serve the world. I am committed to see this happen. We all come from developing nations in the spiritual and moral sense, and we can learn together."

The Japanese government is now much more involved in such matters. For instance, it finances half of the UN High Commission for Refugees (UNHCR) budget for Indochinese refugees and contributes to other UNHCR programs in Asia and Africa. In January 1982, it became the first country in Asia, outside of the Middle East, to accede to the 1951 convention relating to the status of refugees and has a quota of five thousand refugees to be resettled in Japan each year.

Yukika has not rested, however. After the exposure in the early

1990s of widespread corruption among Japanese politicians, bureaucrats, and senior business leaders, she took on yet another task. She started a campaign for clean politics. Her main message to the public is: "If we want to clean up politics, we should start to clean up ourselves first. We cannot only blame the politicians." Now in her eighties, Yukika travels the country, along with the widow of former Prime Minister Miki, appearing widely on television shows and generating considerable coverage in papers and magazines.

Asked by the press where she gets her energy at her age, she says that it comes from a deep desire to see that Japan does not isolate itself from the world, that it learn to care for the world and, in particular, for the children of the world. She sometimes refers to the sad fate of the children left behind in China by Japanese at the end of World War II.

In November 1993, Yukika Sohma received the same Avon Award that had been won by Senator Kato. It was presented to her by Takiko Kato, the senator's daughter. The Avon citation stated, "Ms. Sohma has been engaged for many years in a quest for consistent moral values for mankind, always searching for 'what is right.' She has risked her life in the establishment of democracy and in cleaning up politics and was heavily involved in the realization of peace. She is awarded the prize for her achievements in energetically pursuing justice and the love of mankind." Takiko Kato asked Yukika, "How do you decide *what* is right?" Her reply drew laughter from the celebrities present: "When I consider *who* is right, I always seem to find myself to be right."

Asked at the Avon Award ceremony whether she would have made a difference if she had gone into Parliament—with the implication being that she would have cleaned up politics—she responded strongly, "No, no. The quality of government and of politics reflects the level of responsibility the ordinary citizen takes. We women must face our responsibility for cleaning up society. As wives and mothers of children who will be living in the twenty-first century, we must help usher in a better social and political environment for them."

Yukika wrote at the end of 1993, "I really am grateful with all my shortcomings and my sin for all the chances God has given me to get involved in world events. The interesting tendency in Japan at present is that many young journalists and people concerned with publications are open to the basic idea that 'democracy must start with the change of attitude of ordinary individuals.' It is a chance for Japan to be born anew into a concept of accepting responsibilities and not just clamoring for rights. If every woman started to do what conscience and inspiration impel her to do, we can be a force for true peace and happiness in the world."

Yukika does not regard herself as someone special but says that everyone can do something useful and helpful in the world. Ordinary people who are ready to follow their hearts can do extraordinary things. A journalist who interviewed her for the Avon Award program wrote, "Mrs. Sohma has over the years kept the torch burning to show the way for a just and clean politics and it is up to us to carry on." Yukika simply says, "I get ideas of what should be done, and my friends do them."

11

SISTERS OF COURAGE

*A Colombian ambassador challenges fellow
women to be agents of justice.*

*An Argentinian teacher works to heal the
divisions in her country.*

*A Brazilian activist brings moral and
material advances to her shantytown.*

IN 1992, THE NOBEL PEACE PRIZE was awarded
to Rigoberta Menchú, a Guatemalan Indian of the Quiche tribe,
for her defense of the rights of her people. The Nobel committee
described her as "a vivid symbol of peace and reconciliation across
ethnic, cultural, and social dividing lines, in her own country, on
the American continent, and in the world." She has been called
Sister Courage.

Of her youth, Menchú wrote in her autobiography, *I, Rigoberta
Menchú: An Indian Woman in Guatemala.* "I started thinking about
my childhood and I came to the conclusion that I hadn't had any
childhood at all. I hadn't been to school, I hadn't had enough food
to grow properly, I had nothing." She became a migrant farmhand
at the age of eight and was later employed as a maid in Guatemala
City.

When her father started organizing peasants to resist the appro-
priation of peasant land by wealthy farmers, the family became the
target of attack. Her father, mother, and younger brother were tortured and murdered. In 1982, Rigoberta, who had been working

with her parents, fled to Mexico, where she helped run an activist group, Peasant Unity.

Since the publication of her autobiography in 1983 brought her to the attention of the world community, she has traveled widely in support of human rights and lobbied at the United Nations for indigenous rights. She has to have bodyguards. And her Nobel Peace Prize is not universally applauded in Latin America, where some more educated people resent what they call "Scandinavian interference."

Though not as well known, and with experiences that are less dramatic, there are many other courageous sisters on that continent—some from homes of poverty, others of privilege; some braving violence, others daring to differ with the conventional attitudes of those around them.

One member of the inviting committee for the 1994 Creators of Peace session in Caux was Dr. Heyde Maria Durán de Lopez, from Colombia. Active in Colombia's political life, Heyde has been a government minister with responsibility for the shantytowns, an ambassador representing her country in international negotiations, and a member of the Conservative party. She is prominent in many organizations promoting educational and economic progress, including the National Council of Women, the Association of Business and Professional Women, and the Inter-American Women's Council. She has been vice chair of the Association of Notaries Public, president of the Tribunal of Honor of the Colombian Lawyer's Association, and, in 1988, president of the Colombian Association of Women Lawyers.

Heyde is in many ways typical of the wide range of professional women who feel responsible for the country, whether as doctors, psychiatrists, teachers, or, as in her case, lawyers and politicians. In Bogotá, for instance, most local bank managers are women. In Colombia, women's organizations tend to be strong, efficient, and reliable, she says, "perhaps because it takes a lot more money to corrupt a woman than a man."

Heyde was born in Palmira on March 9, 1939, in the shadow of the Andes Mountains. A bright student, she attended the

Universidad del Externado in Bogotá, three hundred miles to the north, and got her doctorate in law. At the age of twenty, she was already a penal judge in her hometown. At the age of twenty-six, she was the first lawyer to get a dishonest speculator sent to prison. He had been illegally throwing shantytown dwellers off land they had paid for.

Colombia was then just recovering from the ravages of the *violencia,* a bloody civil war (1953–58) that ended in military dictatorship. Feeling a pull to politics, Heyde joined the effort to restore democracy. Family difficulties during these years did not make this easy. First, her mother, who was frail, lived with her, and Heyde had to get up at six, cook lunch, and do everything for her mother before going to the *Capitolio,* where Congress sat. Then she got married to a medical doctor and had a son and two daughters. When she and her husband separated, she had to bring up the children while running an office as a notary public.

On the national scene, Heyde and those around her supported Belisario Betancur, a labor lawyer, in his bid to become president. In 1983, after building a coalition of progressive Conservatives, Christian Democrats, and Anapistas—the party of the former military dictator Rojas—Betancur succeeded in coming to power. Heyde was appointed *secretaria de la presidencia* (junior cabinet minister) for *integración popular,* responsible for the improvement of shantytowns in twenty-two cities around the country. But two years of experience in the forefront of politics were enough for her, and she resigned in disgust. She felt that the president had not given her the support she needed. She returned to her notary public practice, this time in Bogotá.

While attending an international conference in Zipaquirá, outside Bogotá, on the theme "A Meeting of Hope," Heyde reacted vigorously when she heard a priest, Father Miguel Triana, speak. Suddenly, all the resentment she felt against her church welled up in her. Was it not that church, she thought bitterly, that allowed young people to enter marriage without proper preparation and then, when things went wrong, left them in the cold, a church that did not even allow remarriage? But as she tried to listen to the voice in her heart, she heard clearly and surprisingly, "You cannot blame

Heyde Maria Durán de Lopez, as a member of the Colombia house of representatives, speaking up in Parliament in 1970 for greater representation of women in senior government positions and in the political parties. Photograph from the Durán collection.

the church for marrying the wrong man. You said 'yes' to him yourself." She had an honest talk with the priest and was reconciled with the church.

A short time afterwards, her former husband announced to his children that he was coming to Bogotá and was looking for a place to stay. To her surprise, Heyde heard herself saying, "But he can stay with us." As she opened the door to him, she realized that all her hatred against him had gone. Since then they have been able to discuss the future of their children amicably.

As a devout Catholic, Heyde takes as her starting point for

peacemaking the Christian principles enshrined in the Sermon on the Mount. She believes that honest and efficient government flows from the radical application of absolute moral standards, which must begin with each individual. Over the years, her commitment to these principles has deepened, she says, as she has attended conferences like those in Caux and has learned to practice tolerance and forgiveness. A broad ecumenism has enabled her not only to engage in dialogue with those whose political ideas are different from hers but also to build friendships that transcend such differences. When difficulties arise within the family or with employees, she is ready to examine her own behavior with the aim of seeking "the harmony and understanding that should rule in the social world around us." In a society that puts forward the idea that "easy money" is the best way to get ahead, she feels that the younger generation needs quality education that underlines the importance of clear moral guidelines in life.

Colombia is a divided country. Guerrillas and drug terrorists disrupt and bomb their way to power. On one occasion, an unsuccessful car-bomb attempt on the life of the head of security, General Miguel Masa, killed seven passersby and blasted Heyde's Bogotá office. Yet she surprised viewers when she appeared on television full of optimism and without a trace of a vengeful spirit.

In 1990, when she attended a conference on the "Common Moral Search for Peace" in El Salvador, which was then still torn by civil war, she shared her experience of building unity with her political opponents and with political colleagues with whom she had disagreements. "I used to nurse my political hates like plants," she said. "I have stopped watering them, and they have withered. Now I greet these people when I pass them in the street." The challenges of public life in Colombia, including forgiving her enemies, and the act of taking Christ's standards seriously help her "climb the steps of sacrifice and rebirth daily" and "are the best road to God."

In 1991, the old constitution of 1886 was changed with a view to helping end the violence. This purpose was not attained, but the new basic law opened up opportunities for work in the area of civic and ethical values that until then, had been the prerogative of the church. Heyde and her colleagues, for instance, are developing with the Ministry of Education and a Catholic women's lay movement an educational program in this area. She also organized a roundtable with sixteen legislators and educators to discuss values in public life. And she has assembled a large group of professional women who, like herself, have had to deal with separation and coping on their own.

Friends describe Heyde as a dynamo, full of plans, initiatives, and ideas, with a delightful sense of humor and infectious laughter. She has an immense capacity for work and a quick grasp of facts. Heyde gets up early—the moment the sky lights up—to take time to read and think, her one period of peace and quiet. Sometimes she reads the psalms, sometimes the new constitution, and she comes down to breakfast full of ideas. When she has house guests, out comes her china teapot in its cozy basket, bought on her last trip to Hong Kong. "Tea is for conversation," she says. Coffee, one of Colombia's biggest exports, is, presumably, for work.

In 1992, Heyde wrote an article for the alumni magazine of her old school, *Bethlemita de Palmira*, in which she challenged the view that the individual is powerless and asked whether those who lament the immorality in public and private life are doing enough themselves to change it. "You are like all the others and yet created unique," she wrote. "You hold the magic formula in your hands that can change the things you do not like in our society."

She called on her fellow alumni to be agents of justice, starting in the way they treated their families, but also by paying decent wages to their employees, putting their hearts into their work, not cheating. She asked them to help build a community of love where hatred, envy, and resentments were renounced, to put an end to bribery and corruption and dancing around the golden calf. Drawing on her own experience, she wrote, "In most cases we have to start by forgiving: ourselves for what we have done wrong and then with equal largeness of heart 'our enemies.' We have been born into a society convulsed with hate and ambition; may the next generation learn to love and forgive so they can live in peace."

Writing of the need for sincerity, she asked, "Are you honest in your actions, loyal to your children, honest in your business affairs?

Are you aware of the needs of your country when you pay your taxes? If our money is stolen and we begin to steal as well, who is setting an example? Only through honesty can we end the double standard." Writing of the need for generosity that goes beyond those closest to us, and of the wars that have resulted from a minority keeping for themselves what was meant for all, she concluded her article, "A smile, a gift, a generous wage, consoling those who suffer, solidarity. . . . Dear compatriot, stop lamenting and get to work!"

Twenty-five hundred miles to the south is another Catholic woman with a passion for education in a country, Argentina, that is also emerging from years of turmoil. Antonia Caputo de Gallicchio has taught Latin and Spanish grammar and literature in the secondary schools of the capital and province of Buenos Aires and has been at the heart of moves to bring reconciliation between Argentinians and British and between the public at large and those in the military.

Antonia was born in Buenos Aires to Italian parents who, like many Europeans, had come to the country in search of new horizons. Her character, she feels, was much shaped by her parents. Her father was a soldier in Africa for six years around the time of World War I; he was a temperamental man, full of initiative and interested in anything new. Her mother, though possessing a natural intelligence, had had a narrow education; she married young and followed her husband overseas.

A strong cultural foundation was laid when Antonia received a basic Argentine primary school education in the mornings and instruction in Italian language, history, and geography from European teachers in the afternoons. A spiritual foundation was laid first through her family and then reinforced as a teenager. "In the college chapel," she says, "my link with God became a living and lasting experience."

Early on she sensed that she had a gift for teaching, and this inclination, combined with a thirst for reading, led her to study philosophy and literature at the University of Buenos Aires. It was at that time that she met her future husband, Tito. In her last year at the university, her father and Tito's mother both died. The shared sense of loss united the pair in what Antonia calls "a deep sense of life, in the basic values that we were looking for in comradeship and the unity that for us, means marriage." She is grateful that she was able to awaken in Tito religious sentiments that "slumbered in his inmost" and that, with the passage of the years, these have turned into a deep and solid faith to the extent that "now he trusts much more than I in divine providence."

Antonia's many years of teaching experience have convinced her that the ages from fourteen to eighteen are a crucial time in the shaping of a human being and that it is not enough just to pass on information. "I wanted to educate them to aspire to excellence and to be good men and women, to deepen the teaching of what I call the lessons of life." But she also wanted to carry her enthusiasm for teaching to the wider community. "I began to sense," she says, "that the ills that society suffers from are essentially caused by the attitudes we have in daily life."

During a vacation trip to the mountains at Bariloche in the south, the idea was born to set up a meeting place with books and art that could help improve the communal spirit between people. On June 2, 1976, with the help of others, the idea came to fruition with the inauguration of Telus, a house of culture designed by her architect husband in the Belgrano section of Buenos Aires. This was just two months after the coup d'état that deposed Isabel Peron who had succeeded her husband as president of the republic.

It was a terrible time for the country, she recalls. Harsh military men took over from a civilian government that had almost ceased to function. Guerrillas, subversion, armed gangs, killings, people who "disappeared" (*desaparecidos*), were the order of the day. "In this atmosphere I was filled with fear, but all had been planned and could not be postponed. My reason wanted me to stop the project, but my vocation pushed me ahead in spite of everything. The following months seem to prove my reason right. The repression became hard: People were being detained and disappearing. A sculptor who brought us his work was arrested and tortured; two painters who exhibited in Telus went into exile. Culture is always forward looking and is often linked to revolutionary ideas, so it is not surprising that those in power eyed all places of culture with suspicion."

At Telus there were both formal conferences and spontaneous gatherings. Visiting speakers—sometimes people of prominence in the artistic community, such as the writer Ernesto Sábato and the painter Raul Soldi—drew large crowds. The audience, many of whom had to sit on the floor or on the stairs, would listen with respect to these top exponents of Argentine culture. "A real message of the spirit was expressed. People listened with almost religious attention. It was not just showing off famous men and women. The seminars became a refuge in the agitated life of the big city. People did enjoy this spiritual fresh air. There were other moments of friendship and inner peace. There were moments when I felt that my project did meet the essential purpose."

Around 1980, however, the economic situation worsened. In the following year, after her husband was nearly bankrupted by building an apartment block, Telus was closed. With the closing of the house, says Antonia, the vision she had of using her life to improve relationships between people seemed to die too.

In March 1984, when Argentina had just completed its first one hundred days of democracy, Antonia happened upon a conference devoted to peace with the theme, "The Art of Living Together." It was held in an old convent. She had gone there to arrange another meeting, heard all the bustle, asked what was going on, and was invited to attend. It was the day after her only son had entered a seminary to become a priest, and she felt lost. The people who spoke had decided to end the culture of blame and had started to put right what was wrong, starting in their own lives. This made sense to Antonia. The concepts they expressed were no different from the principles of the faith in which she had been brought up, but they sounded different to her. "They made me think more carefully. They meant a more concrete way of practicing my faith. They complemented my beliefs and brought them more to life. The ideal that I thought had died was revived: It was possible to improve relations between people. It was feasible to find inner peace and overcome difficulties and disappointments. But now I understood that I had to start with myself. I used to assume lightheartedly that

Antonia Caputo de Gallicchio and her husband at a conference in 1994 in Petropolis, Brazil, with women from Argentina, Colombia, and Guatemala. Photograph by the author.

I was right and that the others were mistaken. Now I have learned that it may be exactly the opposite and that I have to put myself in my neighbor's shoes to see reality in a more accurate way."

The conference, Antonia discovered, was the second stage of an initiative by another woman in Buenos Aires to bring Argentina and Britain together after their war over the Falkland Islands (Islas Malvinas). She was Ellinor Salmon, a Norwegian-born woman married to an Englishman who had lived in Argentina for forty-five years. A friend of the British community and embassy as well as of leading Argentinians, Ellinor was heartbroken by the war and asked herself, "Why have I not been able to prevent this?" At great risk, Ellinor had decided to work for reconciliation. While Argentina was still under military dictatorship, she had initiated a first international conference to bring Argentinians and British together. The conference attended by Antonia was the second. Thanks to hard work by Ellinor, and finally with the support of former President Arturo Frondizi, visas had been granted for British to attend.

Antonia heard one of them, William Jaeger, say, "We British think we know, but we don't. We believe we are right, but we aren't. We postpone action until it is too late to do what should have been done. We have to build new trust and understanding, starting with change in ourselves."

As it happened, Antonia's younger brother, Dante, was the foreign minister of the newly elected democratic government of President Raul Alfonsin, so she took a group from the conference to meet her brother. A letter from Antonia, describing all she had seen at the conference, was read on national radio. Other radio stations and newspapers picked up the theme of reconciliation. Soon she was involved in ongoing initiatives that led to contacts with Argentine war veterans and a visit by one of them to Britain.

Antonia began to work closely with Ellinor and others not only in this attempt to improve relations between the two countries but also in an effort to heal what she describes as the "open and ever-bleeding wound" of relations then existing between civilians and the military. "We tried to heal the hates and resentments: on the one hand the hates clouding the hearts of the relatives of the young men and women who had been 'disappeared,' and on the other the lack of willingness to admit errors or a lack of repentance for excesses on the part of those who had been in power. After a while we noticed that the wounds were no longer bleeding and appeared to have closed. We do not know whether in full, but a dignified way of living together has been reestablished. We know that what counts is the progress and the change that has been achieved, and we are convinced that we have to continue sowing seeds of friendship, generosity, solidarity, understanding, and honesty."

Antonia has three brothers and values her close and understanding relationship with all of them. She is particularly proud of Dante's work in his six years as foreign minister toward the completion of the Treaty of the Beagle Channel, which, thanks to papal mediation, brought peace between Argentina and Chile when they were on the verge of war. "This urge to harmonize interests through concessions by both contending parties and through dialogue, however straight and severe, has characterized all his national and international policies," both when he served in 1988–89 as president of the UN General Assembly and when he served in 1993 as a negotiator with Haiti for the UN and the Organization of American States (OAS).

Antonia and her brother have the same objectives in life, expressed in their different fields. She says, "We want to soften the sharp edges, shorten the distances between people, and search for common ground, improving human relations, substituting peace for conflict through dialogue and persuasion."

Anna Marcondes Faria, a community leader in the *favelas*, the shantytowns, in Rio de Janeiro, Brazil, comes from a different background from Antonia and Heyde. But, like the women from Argentina and Colombia, she stresses the importance of education in peacemaking. She also shares the conviction of Creators of Peace that besides disarming combatants, peace also means dealing with the causes of hunger and poverty and creating a healthy environment.

Some three million people live in Rio's shacks and shanties that cram every available space around the city, particularly its steep hillsides. Three hundred thousand new people move in each year. Children run wild in the streets. Drug traffickers boast a turnover of $2.5 million a week; sometimes they even have their own uniformed distributors. They try to influence the *favela* associations because they know that they have the power and prestige and can get things done. They want friends in the *favelas* who can warn them when the police are coming or help them get out of prison. *Favela* life is violent. Yet there are women and men of courage, like Anna, who, despite the odds against them, have in the last forty years taken part in what has been described as a do-it-yourself urbanization and one of the great human development stories of our time.

Anna was one of six children born and brought up in a shantytown in the northern part of Rio. Her father was a taxi driver; her mother sewed at home to bring in money for the family. Her mother was religious, her father less so. When she was eight, she was baptized in the Baptist church and, later, was able to get a scholarship from the church that carried her through her first eight years of schooling and enabled her to get training in how to teach religion and how to work with young people.

In her last years at school, Anna met her husband a poor Baptist boy who worked in a brewery. Her father, ambitious for his daughter because of the education she had received, disapproved of their marriage. So they were married in a civil ceremony in 1957. Years later, on their silver wedding anniversary, they would be married in a church. "But over the years," says Anna, "my father had to admit that I had a very excellent husband."

In 1959, the couple moved with their daughter to another *favela*, Parque Vila Isabel, on a nearby hill. Anna finds the name "park" a little ironic. At first they lived in a rented garage, but they had to move because the owner wanted to use it. Then they found one little room on the side of a house; there was no water, electricity, or sewer service, and only a cupboard shoved in front of a doorway provided any privacy. Here five other children, three boys and two girls, were born.

The first electricity they had was obtained by sharing someone else's line, which enabled them to have an icebox, a necessity in Rio's heat. One day after visiting relatives, they came home to find that their neighbor had disconnected the line and the contents of the icebox had spoiled. This led to a quarrel and the realization by Anna that this situation could not go on. "This is how I first got the conviction," she says, "that I needed to do something not only for us but for all the little shacks around us to have light." That was in 1962. When she approached the authorities, she discovered that others were beginning to start *favela* associations in order to fight for better living conditions. This was encouraged by the then governor, Carlos Lacerda. She organized her first meeting in a neighbor's little backyard and founded an association representing the three thousand people who then lived in the *favela*.

At the time, it was rare for a woman to take such initiative. But Anna was fully supported by her husband, who was elected the first president of the association. They had very strict bylaws, she says, governing how they should operate. "The thought was one for all and all for one, that we should not abuse or take advantage of our neighbors. And we began to be very proud of our association." They represented three hills—Flagpole Hill, Garden Hill, and the Banana Garden.

Up until that time, some of those living in the *favelas* had to walk as much as thirty minutes to get water or to wash laundry. Anna and her husband and other elected officials worked hard and persuaded the authorities to provide water for the three hills, which meant installing tanks and pumps. No one received any money for the work that was required. They set up a women's department, which won a number of victories, including the building of small roads connecting the existing main road, Rua Armando de Albuquerque, to the hills. This was the first step in getting electricity to the *favela*. The women's department organized festivals. Since they had little money, they would put oil and wicks into aluminum food tins for illumination. With the money they collected they bought a loudspeaker so that announcements could be made. They arranged courses for the women to learn skills.

One of the biggest lacks was a school for the children. At the time, presidential candidate Marshal Lott promised that he would build a roof for the first school, which was in an old warehouse. He did not win, but he kept his promise anyway. Anna became the school's teacher. She received no pay but was given some bricks so that she could improve her own shack. Later the government made elementary education possible in the *favelas* through radio, and Anna became the radio teacher. The first part of the construction of a more substantial school building on the main street at the bottom of the three hills came through an appeal launched by a television station asking viewers to help provide a kindergarten for every Rio hill.

The association's bylaws required elections every two years, and Anna and her husband filled many positions. But she came to the conclusion that she needed to finish her own high school studies and get a diploma as a teacher. It was difficult, but she did this at night while continuing to take care of the children during the day. With her new skills, she became a teacher in a children's hospital, but in 1970 she resigned from that paid post to set up a kindergarten. "The women were often either single mothers or had husbands who earned very little. They needed to go out to work too, but how could they do that if they had their small children at home? Although I wasn't paid for organizing the kindergartens for our *favelas*, I felt that it was the right thing to do. I felt that God wanted me to do it." The women who had taken the association's courses helped her, though they too needed to get out to do their hairdressing or dressmaking.

When Anna's kindergarten ran into financial difficulties, one woman offered to assume financial responsibility for the school and took it over. But she did not want the volunteer help of the community and charged more than the poorer *favelados* could afford. It still operates, but the price excludes many.

The association started all over again in 1977 with thirty children. They were able to feed the children through help from the state and from mothers who would bring in food. Funding from different state organizations enabled them to build a two-story school building in the *favela* itself. A visiting Rotarian from Los Angeles was so impressed with their dedication that he persuaded his club to help build a third story and a roof.

For many years Anna has been running this kindergarten, now called "The Happy Duckling." One hundred fifty children are registered. Despite difficulties, she has never had to close the kindergarten or leave the children without food. Children attend the day-care center from seven in the morning until five or six in the evening. They are cared for by young women from the *favela*. There is a government-aided preschool under the same roof. Anna also felt the need to lay a sound foundation for the children who go on to the normal city schools and run the risk of being hooked on drugs and becoming street kids. In 1992, she started a community center for youngsters from age seven to seventeen where they can learn cutting and sewing, cooking and baking, sports, hygiene, dancing, and typing—many of the things that could provide a basis for employment. One hundred twenty boys and girls participate and courses are offered in whatever skills the volunteers can teach.

Over the years, Anna and the other *favelados* have sometimes had help from the authorities, sometimes not. "They were years of hard battles." Looking back, she thinks that she was sometimes too

Anna Marcondes Faria (second from left) with three teachers at The Happy Duckling school in 1994. Photograph by the author.

demanding of the young girls who came to help. She has learned, she says, to think first of the people and then of the material things. She regrets that her husband and family may have suffered because of her commitment. There was never the time to make the kind of home she would have liked. "I always had to go out and try to get food for the children for the kindergarten, and there was this lacking and that lacking, and even today I think I did badly by my husband." She still feels the insecurity, and tears come to her eyes as she tells of the struggles. "One of the very hard things, for example, is that our institution gets a city contract in September that is valid for a year and provides the teachers with a minimum salary of eighty to ninety dollars a month. But at the end of the year, you don't know if it is going to be renewed. It is the same with the food for the children and the supplies for those we are trying to train. We are so dependent on different government departments and have no real security."

To Anna, the training of young teachers is vital. "It is important that no selfishness creeps in. It is not just a job but a service to the community. We want to continue that training of thinking for others."

Houses are being improved, with many of them now being built of bricks. There is water, except when the pumps fail, and most houses have electricity, but as yet there are no sewers or drains, just open canals. The three *favelas* have grown tenfold over the years, and there are now, Anna thinks, as many as thirty thousand people living there. "There is still a great deal to be done in the *favelas*. But there is nearly always a tremendous spirit of pulling together, of helping each other, of unity—generally for the good, sometimes for the bad. I and many others in leadership have to continue to work and do our best so that this spirit of generosity, of service, of honesty continues. Step by step the world is opening its heart to our situation; sometimes the most interested are those furthest away."

Financial independence for her work is particularly important to Anna. She would like to create businesses inside the community—perhaps a bakery or a clothes shop—and use income for the school. "We waste a lot of time looking for ways to make money that could be given to the education of our children," she says.

She is determined to provide a proper framework for the children and have the community follow a democratic and a moral course. On one occasion, she was offered a well-paid job outside the *favela*. To the horror of some of her family, she turned it down. "When you accept a job like that," she says, "you are at the command of the politician who gave it to you. I want the freedom to do what I feel is right, and I want to work for our children."

The leadership of women, now more common in the *favelas*, is welcomed. With a few exceptions, they are believed to be less likely than men to use the *favelas* for their own political advancement, and to have a sincere desire to help their communities.

Visitors to Parque Vila Isabel are struck by Anna's serenity and sense of humor amidst the most trying conditions. As she moves around, she is constantly stopped by people with problems and seems to have time for them all. Her own six children have been very supportive of her and are all involved in community work in different Rio *favelas*. Asked how she keeps at peace in her surroundings, Anna says, without elaboration, "I believe in Jesus."

She believes that women have a very important role in peacemaking because of their peacemaking activities in the family. Peace begins with peace with God, she says, and is a quality of life you can pass on only if you possess it yourself. "When the family has peace it spreads to the community." She sees her work as helping children to escape both from the spirit of bitterness and from the influence of an evil environment. By learning a trade, a child is less likely to be violent, to be a thief, to go around mugging people. One of the young men she taught to read and write is now a *favela* leader. "It is a great joy when you see that he has taken the right road," she says.

12

HOMESICK
ELEPHANTS

*To monarch or missionary, to prime minister
or peasant, this Burmese educator displayed
the same humor and directness.*

"I QUITE FELL IN LOVE with her," said Mahatma
Gandhi about Burmese educator Daw Nyein Tha, who once visited him at his ashram in Wardha.

At age twenty-one, Ma Mi, as she was affectionately known, was the youngest headmistress in Burma, now renamed Myanmar by its present leaders. She went on to become a world citizen, received in homes large and small, from villagers' huts in Asia to the palaces of the king of England and the president of India. She spoke to audiences as varied as members of the League of Nations at a meeting in Geneva and thirty thousand Americans in the Hollywood Bowl. Two things made an encounter with her unforgettable: her profound faith that God could speak to any individual who was ready to obey, and her skill at communicating simply and graphically that a change in the world had to start with the way you lived your own life. Brought up a Christian in a Buddhist land, Ma Mi constantly moved toward a deeper understanding of herself and others, discovering that in the practical reality as well as in the ideal, there is, in the end, no division when faith is lived.

"Go and see Gandhiji." "Give this message to Aung San." "Resign." "Stay one year." Often the thoughts she got were most explicit—and were obeyed. Indeed, in the Burmese language, to listen and to obey are the same—*na taung ba*. She never limited her concerns to one issue or one country and, appropriately, her biography by Marjorie Procter is called *The World My Country*. The key, according to Ma Mi, was "accepting the place where God put me as [if it were] my country, because it belongs to him, and not keep longing to go back 'home.'"

While making the world her country, however, Ma Mi did not let her love for her own country and her desire for it to play a diplomatic role be diminished. In her later years, she sensed the wrong turn Burma was taking and was saddened when the Burmese military government refused to reissue her passport. As one who fought an unrelenting battle for government incorruptibility and democracy, she would have been deeply shocked at the continuing dictatorship in that great land. But she would have been delighted at the award of the Nobel Peace Prize to Aung San Suu Kyi, whose family she had known for years. Today, despite her party winning 392 out of 485 seats in the first multiparty elections in twenty-six years, Suu Kyi has been kept under house arrest since July 20, 1989. Ma Mi would have been concerned for Suu Kyi's safety and well-being and impressed by her conviction that love is the answer to fear and that the Burmese people should demonstrate the capacity to forgive.

Suu Kyi's father, General Aung San, is revered as the father of his country. In his daughter's words he "constantly demonstrated courage—not just the physical sort but the kind that enabled him to speak the truth, to stand by his word, to accept criticism, to admit his faults, to correct his mistakes, to respect the opposition, to parley with the enemy, and to let the people be the judge of his worthiness as a leader."

General Aung San once told Ma Mi that when he was quite young he discovered that he was afraid to go to the graveyard at night. "I cannot have this fear in me," he thought. "It must go." So, in the middle of the night, he went to the graveyard, and lit a candle, and when he had returned home, his fear had gone. "Fear is a very wrong thing," he told Ma Mi.

When Ma Mi was fourteen years old, her headmistress at the Morton Lane School in Moulmein told her that if she passed all her examinations she could one day become the school's headmistress. Ma Mi prayed, "Lord, if you will let me pass my exams in three years, I will serve you for the rest of my life." She said later that it was just the promise of a little girl who wanted to pass an examination, but she kept the promise. In 1921, after obtaining her teaching diploma at Judson College, she did, indeed, become the headmistress of her old school with 650 girls. After ten years there, a stormy clash developed with students and staff because of her authoritarian ways. It was resolved when she faced up to the fact that the issue was not who was right or wrong but that she had hated the girls and that her pride and conceit had made it difficult for the staff to work with her. She apologized to the girls and to the teachers and, in doing so, learned a lesson for life. "My whole relationship with the girls and the teachers, and the atmosphere in the school, became different," she said. "Now I knew why Christ put me in this school—not just to be headmistress, but to learn to love people."

In 1931, she was invited by the widely respected missionary E. Stanley Jones, author of the best-selling book, *The Christ of the Indian Road*, to join a four-month campaign in India and then to go to Britain on a mission of fellowship. This mission came out of a recommendation of the International Missionary Council, meeting in Jerusalem in 1928, that "the younger churches in the mission field should be invited to share with the older churches what they had learned of God through Jesus Christ."

Ma Mi traveled to the principal cities of Britain, spending a week in each. Ma Mi, a Baptist, was given permission by the archbishop of Canterbury, William Temple, to preach in Anglican churches. She spoke at the London School of Divinity and in her own denomination's Spurgeon's Tabernacle. She also addressed a large public meeting in Westminster Hall, chaired by Archbishop Temple. She was sitting with the other Asians in the front row, and some twenty bishops sat behind them. After the meeting, she was asked if she had been fearful with twenty bishops behind her. She replied that, being a Baptist, she had not known that she should be afraid of a bishop.

The archbishop, who hosted her in his home, said, "Thank you for what you gave at the public meeting; you have helped an old sinner like me." "It wasn't me," she said later. "Every time I spoke I asked God to tell me just what to say, and that touched the archbishop."

On this visit she was received by King George V and Queen Mary at Buckingham Palace. At the time, Burma no longer wanted political separation from India under the British Raj. "What is this I heard about you?" the king asked her. "I thought you wanted separation, and what is this now?"

"Your Majesty," she replied, "whether we are politically separated or not, we should all work together for the Kingdom of God. And what we are doing here is it."

On this 1932 visit, she also met men and women from the Oxford Group (the forerunner of MRA, see page 171), a powerful movement of religious awakening. They introduced her to a further growth in her faith and to the thought that when people listen, God speaks, and when they obey, he acts.

On returning to Burma in 1933, she went to teach at the Women's Bible Training School and traveled with the Burma Gospel Team throughout the country and to Malaysia, Singapore, and Indonesia. Then came an invitation to leave city life and live in the up-country village of Thamin-in-Gon. It was a test of her commitment. She was used to servants and sanitation and a car to get about in, but she felt that it was right to accept the invitation and went for a year. She said of her time at Thamin-in-Gon that she had "no companionship, no mental stimulus, often a meal of rice and an egg, never knowing where the next rupee was coming from, no medical knowledge, no training, and the dead weight of ignorance and inertia all around—but always God. God for companionship, for information, for courage, for strength." Her love for the villagers came to outweigh the discomforts she had to put up with.

One result, according to her biographer, was that "forever after villages were written on her heart, the villages of Burma, the teeming villages of India and of all Asia. She knew that they were the lifeblood of a country. Although she never again lived for so long as this in any village, she loved to visit them in Burma and elsewhere" (p. 32).

Fresh from her experience in that remote village, Ma Mi returned to England in 1935 to an Oxford Group assembly, where she got to know the men and women from Asia and around the world that she would work with for the rest of her life. They included the newly appointed Anglican bishop of Rangoon, George West. In the next months she was in Europe, America, and Asia, often speaking to large audiences about her experiences. She became part of a new spirit permeating Burma that was uniting Baptists and Anglicans, Christians and Buddhists, Karens and Burmans (minority and majority communities), British and Burmese.

On Burmese National Day in 1939, her friend Bishop West was asked to propose a toast to Burma and she was asked to respond at a dinner in Rangoon attended by three hundred dignitaries and broadcast to the nation. It was just after the government had issued a report on widespread bribery and corruption. Bishop West said, "We can make this national day not only a day of celebration, but the launching of a nationwide campaign against personal and communal selfishness."

Ma Mi replied in her characteristic style: "This is the beginning of a new era of national unity and freedom. Some of us like to think our troubles are very complicated. Actually they are very simple. What is the answer to all this dishonesty? The answer to dishonesty is—an honest man. I would like to see honesty walking about on two feet. Gentlemen, may I remind you, you all have two feet. There is nothing complicated about absolute honesty. It's just a matter of being absolutely honest in everything with everybody all the time. Some of us are partly honest with some people some of the time. We do not want people who are moderately honest, who reject most of the bribes. Who wants to draw most of his salary? To eat an egg that is moderately good? To live in a house that keeps out most of the rain? To travel in a ship that floats most of the time? I'm talking about honesty not because it is the only quality we need but because it's basic. We can't build a house on rotten posts. The trouble with us is that we are an individualistic people. Look at the word *individualistic*: five *i*'s and one *u*. Look at the word *unity*: One *u* and one *i* and the *u* comes first."

As a teacher, Ma Mi had a fund of interesting and simple ways of expressing timeless truths that captivated audiences all over the world. "Why do we need to change?" she would ask. "How many of us washed our hands this morning? Didn't you wash your hands ten years ago? Didn't you wash your hands last week? Why, then, did you wash your hands this morning? Because we use our hands all the time, we need to wash them all the time, and sometimes more than once a day. In the same way we need to keep our hearts clean all the time. Through our eyes, our ears, our minds, things go into our hearts. Therefore we need to keep our hearts clean, just as we keep our hands clean, all the time.

"We are like pools of water—clear, sparkling water, and everyone comes to drink from it and goes away refreshed with new life. Then one little leaf falls—it floats on the top and goes down to the bottom. And another little leaf falls. And so they come, one after the other. You look at the pool. The top looks clean and clear . . . but stir it up and see how all the leaves come up. Would you like to drink that water now? Why, you wouldn't even wash your clothes in it. So the only thing to do is to clean the whole thing and put in fresh water."

Her simple-sounding illustrations were backed by practical experiences of change in her own life: the reconciliation with her pupils and staff back at the school where she was the headmistress; the way she overcame a broken engagement; her determination not to hate the Karens, the Chinese, or the Japanese. At a meeting with a group of missionaries where she had spoken on the subject of sin, one missionary said, "My sins have all been forgiven."

"What sins?" asked Ma Mi.

"Sin in general," the missionary replied.

"I do not know 'sin in general,'" said Ma Mi. "My sins are all specific."

In 1941, Ma Mi had what she thought was a ridiculous thought: to go and see Mahatma Gandhi. Within days she was at his ashram at Wardha. At the end of evening prayers, Gandhi greeted her. "You have come to see me?" he asked.

"Yes, God sent me to you," she replied.

"Have you had any supper?"

"Not yet."

"Then come along with me."

After he had given her supper, he said, "Now tell me what God said to you."

"Mr. Gandhi, God told me to tell you to call Asia back to to him."

"That is a very difficult thing for one man to do," he said. "I don't know how to do it. Not even India listens to me."

She told him many stories of her travels, and how her traveling expenses were paid, and how she had found that anyone—whatever their race or creed—would listen to a wisdom greater than their own, that absolute moral standards were a good test of thoughts to see whether they were really God's guidance.

"I have just had guidance," said Gandhi mischievously.

"What is it?" asked Ma Mi.

"Half of everything you get you give to me!" laughed the Mahatma.

He asked her how long she could stay.

"Mr. Gandhi, my work is done," she said. "I must go back tomorrow morning."

"You must come back and stay here with me as long as possible."

"When God sends me back, I shall be most happy to come."

"We all go to bed at 8:30," said Gandhi. "Now, we sleep on the ground. It is the finest bed in the world. There is room for everybody. Mother Earth. Where would you like to sleep? On the ground or on a cot?"

"Mr. Gandhi sleeps on the ground. I'll sleep on the ground too."

"No, no, we can easily find you a bed."

"Really, I'd just as soon have the ground," she insisted.

"What was the first standard you told me about?" Gandhi asked.

"Absolute honesty," she replied.

"Now, remembering that standard, which would you rather have, the ground or the cot?"

"The cot," Ma Mi admitted.

"You see, the difficulty with you," Gandhi said to Ma Mi, "is, you only know what God tells you. I hear what the devil says too."

The next morning Gandhi told her, "If you ever come to India

Daw Nyein Tha (second from left) with Daw Mya Yee (wife of then Prime Minister U Nu), Daw Khin Kyi (widow of General Aung San), and Buddhist monk U Narada outside Rangoon's Aletawaya Monastery in 1956. Photograph by David Channer.

again, you must come and stay with me." Later he sent her a card with the words, "I do try to listen to God and obey him with all my heart."

During World War II, Ma Mi's "adventures in obedience," as she called them, were put to the test as she and fellow villagers went through extraordinary privations and had narrow escapes in evading the Japanese after they invaded Burma in 1941. She had the sense of being preserved to help in the reconstruction of Burma through the reconstruction of its people. She also felt even before the war ended that Aung San had a key role to play in an independent Burma. She and Bishop West and those working with them believed that he could be a unifying force for the country. "Take this message to Aung San," was the compelling thought she had. Before long, they were meeting with him to plan for the country.

In 1946, on the first National Day after the Japanese occupation, Ma Mi was invited to broadcast to the nation. She said, "As *Bogyoke* [General] Aung San has called us to meet the challenge of our times, we must all together have the privilege of rising to the challenge. The call will be—as every right call always is—to sacrifice. The appeal to self-interest is out-of-date. That appeal has destroyed cities, created havoc, and ruined a civilization. The call is to build. We want no utopia. We want to pioneer in the great adventure of finding out how to apply at all times, in all circumstances, the great privilege of democracy, which is also a law of life—all for each and each for all."

Ma Mi also broadcast on the day the Karen community celebrated its New Year's Day. She spoke forcefully, as a Burman, of her deep appreciation of the Karen community and of the role it could play in the country.

At the end of 1946, Aung San told Ma Mi and her friends that his war career was over and that he would never again take part in any armed conflict. The country, however, was in turmoil. Strong passions had been unleashed: in some areas the Communists, in others the Karens or the government, were in control. But there was no fighting in the half dozen villages in the Kappali area, where Ma Mi's friends had helped the Burmese, Karens, and English work together. This was a time, too, of widely publicized corruption. So came the thought, "Invite Aung San to Kappali."

The general, who as deputy chairman of the governor's executive council, was already the effective prime minister of Burma, had heard stories coming out of Kappali, a village peopled by Karens, Burma's largest minority. They were developing an answer to corruption: If no one gives a bribe, no one can receive a bribe. Enough villagers had stopped giving bribes that bribery was losing its grip in the area. Aung San decided to accept the invitation and see for himself.

It was vacation time, so Ma Mi, who had returned to her school in Moulmein as superintendent, was able to join the general and his wife, who had been one of her pupils. "All along the route, people were waiting for Aung San," said Ma Mi. "They waved and sang and greeted him. There were about twenty parties dancing for him. There was a lovely breakfast laid out, and it was like this everywhere, one big crowd after another. As we came to the village, thirty thousand people were waiting. They welcomed him with more songs and dances and flowers."

A huge *pandal* (awning) had been constructed under which fifteen thousand closely packed people could be accommodated on the mat flooring. A platform had been erected at one end for the guests of honor. The general took his place, wearing a multicolored "Karen jacket," a gift of the people of Kappali to their Burmese leader. The Karen villagers were proud to see their leader—a Burman, whose forebears had fought the Karens—wearing their traditional jacket.

Before Aung San spoke, headmen from the nearby villages, where the "revolution of character" had spread, came in a procession. One by one they put their names on what they called a "village charter." Normally, when a prime minister visited an area, it was customary to present some sort of a demand—for a new road, a new school, or a deeper river canal. But this was a promise to receive no more bribes, to give no more bribes, to administer the villages justly, and to work with the Burmese.

Marjorie Procter writes in *The World My Country*:

> People came not only to hear General Aung San but also to tell him about the change that had taken place in their lives, which affected all that they did. Debts were disappearing, private feuds, their fear and hatred of the Burmese, their fear of government officials, especially the police. They were experimenting with new crops, doing better with old ones, and it was easier to keep their village paths and bridges in order. They cooperated better and worked with a will. They were happier, and they wanted to put all that they had discovered at the disposal of other villages. (p. 85)

The Burmese leader had not seen anything like it before. Deeply moved, he said, "This is what I want for all of Burma." Sadly, he did not live to see it. On July 19, 1947, gunmen burst into the government offices in Rangoon where the Burmese leaders were meeting and started firing. When they stopped, Aung San and seven of his cabinet were dead. Aung San's widow, Daw Khin Kyi, stepped forward, determined that her own loss would not impede the country's progress. She asked that there be no weeping in her house. For the sake of the children, she said, there must be no crying or bitterness. "My husband loved them so and planned for them. What could they grow up to be if they had crying and bitterness now."

The bodies of Aung San and his cabinet lay in state in Jubilee Hall, and every day Daw Khin Kyi visited the hall to see that all was in order. "I have moved the wreaths around," she said. "There are too many on his coffin and not enough on the others. I divided them up evenly. My husband knew how to build a team for the country, and so he even died with his team." She visited the homes of the other widows. To them she said, "Why are you crying? Is it that you want your husbands back to serve you or is it that you can no longer serve them? If so, I can tell you that I shall continue to serve my late husband by serving my country and carrying on the work that he started. I am going to put my name forward for the legislature. How about you?"

Daw Khin Kyi did so and was elected, becoming minister of health and later ambassador to India. And it was in India, as a fifteen-year-old, that her daughter, Suu Kyi, studied the life of the Mahatma from whom she derived her nonviolent philosophy.

Ma Mi was able to speak of the work of Aung San at the Caux conference and later to welcome Daw Khin Kyi there. She met their two surviving children, Aung San U and Suu Kyi, later in England. A third child had drowned when he was eight.

At one point, Ma Mi had a hand in settling a long-standing dispute between Burma and neighboring Thailand. This dispute went back to 1767, when a Burmese king had invaded Thailand and burned the cultural and commercial center of Ayudhya. It centered around white elephants, which were highly prized in both countries as symbols of power and royalty. They also had a religious dimension, as the Gautama Buddha was said to have spent one of his preexistences as a white elephant, and the hunt for these prized mammals led to cross-border forays.

In 1954, Ma Mi was in Thailand for a conference. Wherever

"When I point my finger at my neighbor, there are three more pointing back at me." —Daw Nyein Tha in the early fifties. Photograph by Guy Woolford.

she went, she noticed that the wars with Burma were recalled in writings and monuments. She had taught history and had not even known of these wars; Burmese history had focused on the struggle with Britain. As she was due to be presented to the Thai prime minister, she asked God what to say. The thought came to take him a small seed, such as can be bought in a bazaar. In its hollowed-out interior were three minute white ivory elephants.

"Your air force has been bombing our villages and they've killed some of our people," Prime Minister Pibul Songgram said to her. "I wrote to your prime minister about it and he hasn't answered."

Ma Mi apologized for what her countrymen had done and said that she was sure it wasn't intentional. Then she knelt before the prime minister, unwrapped the paper, shook the tiny elephants out of the seed into the palm of her hand, and held it out to him. "These little elephants have been away from Thailand for such a long time, nearly two hundred years," she said. "They were so homesick, they have gone very thin."

The prime minister laughed. Afterwards he told a journalist about the gift of elephants from a Burmese woman, and the story went out on the radio. He also ordered an end to anti-Burmese broadcasts on the Thai radio.

On her return home, Ma Mi told her own prime minister what she had heard, and he apologized over the radio for what Burma had done. In April 1955, the Burmese prime minister visited Thailand on his way to the Afro-Asian summit in Bandung. At a reception, he apologized publicly to the prime minister and to the people of Thailand for what Burma had done in the past. Handing over a check toward the repair of the ruins of Ayudhya and compensation for the villagers who had suffered in the bombing incident, he said, "Even though our generation was not responsible for it, we accept full responsibility."

All her life, Ma Mi was frugal and disciplined in the use of money, and yet she always trusted that God would meet her needs. On one occasion she presented herself to the American consul to get a visa for the United States. The consul wanted to know how she would support herself there. "Do you have fifty dollars?" he asked.

"No, I'm sorry," she said.

"What are you going to do in America then?"

"God will provide."

"Come, come," the consul said, "the streets here are crowded with people for whom God is not providing."

"I know, but God will provide for me."

"I'd like to have a certificate to that effect," he remarked.

So she told him of all the gifts of money she had received to pay for her ticket.

Ma Mi died at Asia Plateau, the conference center in India established by Mahatma Gandhi's grandson, Rajmohan. There a room is named in her honor. Irene Laure, who was at Asia Plateau when she died, called Ma Mi "the best ambassador of Burma anywhere in the world."

One of Ma Mi's remarks has now become currency the world over—a Burmese saying that she always accompanied with expressive gestures: "When I point my finger at my neighbor, there are three more pointing back at me." One of her most expressive visual demonstrations appears in a film about Mary McCleod Bethune's life, *The Crowning Experience*: "Do you know what causes tension?" she asked holding up a handkerchief. "Look, when I insist," she said, pulling on one corner, "and you resist," pulling on the opposite corner, "see the tension." "When I want my way and you want your way, there is tension between us. If I insist strongly enough and you resist strongly, there is bound to be a break and we grow further apart.

"Now if I don't insist," she said as she stopped pulling with one hand, "then you can't resist." And the handkerchief fell loosely. Then, bringing the corners together, she said, "We can both assist. When we both get back to God and want only what is right, then we are united."

When she demonstrated this for Mahatma Gandhi in his mud hut, he responded, "Yes, it works very well with the handkerchief. But does it work with people?"

Her lifelong friend Bishop West said, "Ma Nyein Tha's greatness was that she made it work with people."

13

THE OTHER SIDE
OF THE COIN

*An Egyptian doctor seeks common ground
between faiths.*

*A Jewish refugee from war-torn Europe works
quietly behind the scenes.*

ON SEPTEMBER 13, 1993, leaders of Israel and of the Palestine Liberation Organization (PLO) signed a declaration of principles on interim Palestinian self-government. The handshake between Prime Minister Yitzhak Rabin and PLO Chairman Yasir Arafat at the ceremony at the White House in Washington, D.C., surprised and inspired the world community. Careful, innovative work behind the scenes by a few Norwegians had laid the foundation for an event that most people in the Middle East—and in the world at large—never expected to see in their lifetime. The BBC "Panorama" program said that the "Norwegian channel" had "proved that goodwill and friendship can change the course of history."

At the White House signing, President Clinton said that the declaration of principles "charts a course towards reconciliation between two peoples who have both known the bitterness of exile. Now both pledge to put old sorrows and antagonisms behind them and to work for a shared future shaped by the values of the Torah, the Qur'ān, and the Bible." He also said that "a peace of the brave"

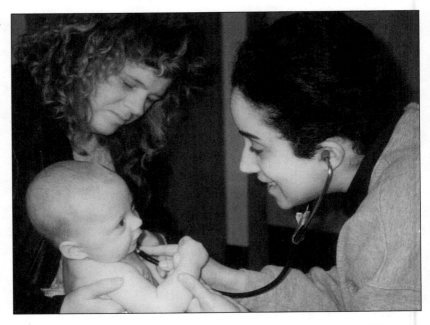

Omnia Marzouk at work in a clinic of the British National Health Service. Photograph by Pauline MacLachlan.

was within reach, despite "those who still prefer the easy habits of hatred to the hard labor of reconciliation."

The U.S. president said, "Let the skeptics of this peace recall what once existed among these people. There was a time when the traffic of ideas and commerce and pilgrims flowed uninterrupted among the cities of the fertile crescent. In Spain, in the Middle East, Muslims and Jews once worked together to write brilliant chapters in the history of literature and science. All this can come to pass again."

A young Egyptian doctor, Omnia Marzouk, watching the events on television, felt amazement and hope mixed with concern and apprehension: "Amazement and hope at the sight of two very courageous men, Rabin and Arafat, shaking hands. They had decided to make a complete psychological break from the prevailing attitudes of their peoples' long-suffering history. Concern and apprehension about the very difficult road ahead from this statement of principles to a negotiated and complete settlement. To build a real and lasting peace, people will have to look back and find healing from the great pain and anguish of the past. It will be very painful for those concerned and for those of us who care for people on both sides of the conflict. For that we will need all our skills as listeners, including confidentiality; we will need to be shock absorbers and share in the deep pain. We will all need to be channels so that our individual friendships can bring about a change in individual lives."

Omnia, who now works as a pediatrician in Liverpool, England, has traveled more than many of her compatriots, but she may be typical of a younger generation of Arabs faced with the challenges of a changing world. Her experience also underlines the key premise of Creators of Peace: that effectiveness begins at a personal level, with the standards you accept for your life.

Omnia's father was a career diplomat who served as ambassador in the Seychelles, Kenya, Fiji, New Zealand, and Australia. She has spent equal amounts of time in Egypt, Australia, and Britain. She attended primary school in Cairo and then in Canberra, where her father opened the first Egyptian embassy in 1960. She started attending high school in Cairo but spent her last two years in Canberra, when her father returned as ambassador. She told a meeting in Cardiff City Hall in 1991, "I am a Muslim and I am proud of my Muslim, Egyptian, and Arab cultural traditions, but I am also lucky to have been greatly enriched by living in the Western Christian world through my father's career as a diplomat and more recently through my own work as a doctor in Britain. As a result I feel called to be a bridge between Islam and the West."

As a child, Omnia remembers the Arab-Israeli war of 1967, with blackouts, air raids, and the hysterical crying of other schoolchildren who had fathers in the army. Her trip out to Australia occurred during the October 1973 war. All Egyptian ambassadors who had just been appointed had to leave for their posts immediately in order to present the government's position. Her father and the family took a roundabout route from Cairo to Tripoli, then to

Saudi Arabia and Hong Kong. They arrived exhausted twenty-four hours later in Sydney, where her father had to give an immediate press conference about the war.

Omnia was sixteen when she experienced her first bomb threat. Answering the phone in her home in Canberra, she heard someone shouting insults about the Arabs and saying that "a bomb will go off in the house in a few minutes." Her father was away at the time, so she told her mother. They walked into the garden of the embassy residence. "I thought I'd better tell the policeman who guarded the Russian embassy next door. A few minutes later we just went on with what we had been doing. I remember thinking how strange that someone wanted to threaten and kill us simply because we were Arabs."

The press stereotypes of the Muslim world that she encountered—depicting uncultured and wealthy Arabs, unprovoked terrorists, and oppressed and uneducated women—did not correspond to any of the people she knew or her family and friends. She and her brother, for instance, were treated the same, and the expectation was that both would combine professional and family lives. "I had subconsciously begun to believe that to be modern and live in this century I had to be more Western."

Omnia feels that she was fortunate to attend a family camp for university students and young working people at Stanwell Tops, south of Sydney, and to meet young men and women who had a quality of life and an honesty that challenged her to look more deeply into her own faith, its culture, and heritage and to begin to pray regularly, an integral part of Muslim belief. "I began to see how important a base faith is for day-to-day life," she says. "I saw more clearly that the knowledge and technological advance that I wanted to gain from my Western education did not have to be at the expense of faith and morality. I did not have to become more Western to be modern; I could choose the progress but still adhere to my faith. I did not have to go down the road of moral disintegration that I saw around me in the West."

Her journey of faith had been dramatically encouraged by meeting Christians in Australia who lived their faith. It seemed natural to her that in a multifaith world, people of faith should encourage one another to live up to the best of their respective faith's teachings. As she started at Sydney University in 1976, she made three decisions: never to drink alcohol; to make friends with people of both sexes but not to have an exclusive or sexual relationship with any man; and to help Christians live their faith in the same way that her new Christian friends had helped her live hers.

She lived in a Methodist college residence that housed men and women and where alcohol and easy relationships were the norm, but although fully involved in all aspects of college life, she kept to her decisions. "I was one of the few students who didn't drink when I started at the college, but five years later when I left, our numbers had grown. I was, however, one of the only ones who never had any drinks spiked by the hardened drinkers." In her last year, she was nominated by the students to represent them and received a scholarship for her sporting and academic achievements and contributions to college life—the first woman to be so honored since the college had admitted women ten years earlier.

In 1979, Omnia made her first visit to Caux as one of a delegation of Egyptian students who were part of a British-Arab university exchange program. Arriving late at night, they were offered supper. As the food was laid on the table, she was told that a special dish that contained no pork would be ready for her in a moment. Muslims are forbidden to eat pork. "I remember being bowled over by the fact that in this huge place with more than four hundred people attending the conference, someone somewhere had given thought to such a small detail. It summed up the spirit of care for people no matter who they were that I felt needed to be multiplied in the world to make it a better place for everyone."

Omnia points to three areas of common ground among people of faith on which to build. The first is the fact that all faiths recognize the need for absolute moral standards. The second is that in every faith there is a seeking for divine wisdom, whether the source is called God, Allah, Yahweh, or the Inner Voice. As do other Muslims, Omnia prays five times a day, reciting the opening *sura* (chapter) of the Qur'ān, which is like the Lord's prayer for Christians and includes the phrase "show us the right path." "It means," she says "that there must be a two-way process—not just praying, but also asking God to show us in our day-to-day decisions how faith is meant to be relevant." The third area of agreement is the concept that faith is not just a personal matter but something you draw on to change the things in society that need to be changed.

Omnia regards her decision to make faith central in her life and to seek God's direction in studies, career, work, where and how she lives, and what she does with money as a key to effective bridge building between communities. She expects to take the initiative and not wait for others, to build a climate of trust with different peoples within her own local setting, within her own region of the Middle East, and in the world. She is fortunate, she says, to be part of the National Health Service, Europe's largest employer, where people of different backgrounds are working together. Her skills in language and in building relationships with patients, their families, and colleagues are an essential part of peace creation. Her two best friends at her hospital are a Ghanaian Methodist and an Irish Catholic; the professor who started her on her research work is a South African Jew; there is a Buddhist technician and a Hindu—and all these are in just one department. "As you start to build simple friendships with people you begin to feel free enough to ask questions about their faith; you begin to acquire facts and blow out of your mind all the stereotypes that you have accumulated over the course of your lifetime. This is a great exercise and is the first step in acquiring facts about another faith."

It would be easy, as foreign doctors, to band together, but Omnia makes it a point to reach out; she is interested in people as friends. By answering their questions, she hopes to remove some of the misunderstandings about Arabs, the Muslim world, and especially the role of women in Islam. "When people ask her questions during Ramadan (the annual period of daytime fasting) or when she takes time out at the hospital to do her prayers, she hopes that her answers help people see a different picture.

During a busy on-call shift during one Ramadan, one of Omnia's colleagues offered to come in for an hour to allow her to break the fast. "It meant a great deal to me that she appreciated my efforts but also respected my decision to observe my faith practices." And when Ramadan comes to an end, Omnia's Ghanaian and Irish colleagues and others join her in celebrating. Indeed, each of them also gives up something while she fasts.

Omnia seems to take the occasional prejudice she encounters with a certain detachment and considerable grace—whether it is a prejudice against foreigners or questions about where she did her training because of her "funny-sounding name." Some of these prejudices, she feels, reflect a misplaced sense of superiority. "I don't face as much of this as other foreign doctors," she says. "People are usually dumbfounded when I start to talk English with an Australian accent!"

She has had what she calls some "rather amusing experiences." One woman came into the emergency department wanting an opinion on her children's problems. When Omnia asked why she had not gone to her own general practitioner, the woman answered that he was a "foreign GP." On one occasion, a colleague wanted to consult with the resident of another specialty team about a child she had been asked to evaluate. When the list of available consultants turned out to be all seemingly foreign names, she asked whether there wasn't a nonforeign resident she could speak to. Suddenly seeing Omnia, she said, "You know I didn't mean anything against you. I just wanted to talk to someone competent."

In her research work in 1988–90, Omnia was assessing children in seven hospitals who had a particular type of meningitis and septicemia (blood infection). Her approach was to recognize that she was on a steep learning curve and "to listen to everyone, to be prepared to learn from anyone, to be totally available, to be ready to be just an extra pair of hands when needed, and to make suggestions only when asked." This overcame the natural suspicions of medical and nursing staff toward so-called outside experts, who have a tendency to come in and tell them what to do without appreciating their unique situation.

Omnia says that the challenge to live one's faith and to be a bridge builder in the modern world is the same for all. For example, the challenge to live honestly means that if she goes on a trip while doing hospital work, she does not claim expenses that are not related to that work; and she is strict in using the hospital photocopier only for hospital work. "These are simple decisions that I have to make as a Muslim living on the basis of honesty, but someone who is Christian goes through the same process."

Another challenge she cites is the basis of relationships with other people. Amidst all the talk of "safe sex," she believes, as a Muslim, that people should also be told, "no sex until marriage." She knows that she is up against a strong tide of opinion going the other way and counts on people of faith to help one another hold to the highest standards. "People of other faiths who stand up for their beliefs and practices encourage me to live out my faith."

A further aspect in building bridges, she says, is the ability to not only understand the facts about someone else's faith but also live into their fears, hurts, and bitterness, which are a legacy of history and still affect interfaith dialogue today. Her eyes and heart were opened to this dimension at an interfaith dialogue at Asia Plateau in India in 1991.

She went to that dialogue with a mixture of reactions that had accumulated over the preceding six months. Deep feelings smoldered in her about the Gulf War. She felt hurt because of the world's negative reaction or indifference to the Arab world, angry at the folly of Arab actions, shame at the suffering that Arabs were inflicting on one another, and overwhelmed by questions she was asking about her faith. "Did it have to take a war before you did so?" she thought.

As a doctor she was conscious of the cost in human lives and felt equally for the 100,000 Iraqis and the fifty coalition soldiers who had died. She wondered why in the twentieth century we had not developed better skills in diplomacy and negotiation. "I realized that it was no longer a question of expressing how I felt but was I prepared to live differently enough to bring about reconciliation and healing? Was I prepared to do more to build bridges of understanding between people?" Omnia realized that to do so she had to be free of her anger, resentments and fears. She had tried everything humanly possible to be free of these feelings and had to pray for God to free her from them.

Being in India at this time helped her. She faced the fact that when the Muslim Moghuls had invaded India they had left in their trail, in the name of Islam, a heritage of hurts and wrong deeds that continued to inflame the divisions and conflicts in modern India. During the Gulf War, too, innocent civilians in Israel and Saudi Arabia were being subjected to Scud missiles. "As I looked at all the hurt and resentment, I felt suddenly aware that there are times in history when we were the people causing hurt to other people; and that there were also people in the West who felt hurt and angry about their encounters with the Muslim world. I saw the other side of the coin. In addition to feeling your own hurts and those of your own people, you have to identify with the hurts that have been inflicted by your group on other people. On that basis we are all equal, and none of us can stand up and say that we are blame-free."

She told the dialogue, "I feel deeply sorry for those who have been hurt and have suffered at the hands of Arabs or Muslims for whatever reason or been hurt by their contact with them. I apologize to those here who have been hurt by such contacts."

Omnia believes that the greatest need in the world as the next century approaches is for people who are different to learn to work together. For her, any attempts to bridge the gaps of misunderstanding, misconceptions, and fears must start with simple friendships. "If we all stopped talking about the theory," she says, "and actually lived our faiths, we would be surprised by our ability to learn from one another and by the extent to which our lives are enriched by our diversity. At the level of a life lived there is nothing that divides us." She likes to quote a *sura* from the Qur'ān: "We [God] . . . have made you nations and tribes that ye may know one another [and be friends]. The noblest of you in the sight of Allah, is the best in conduct." And another *sura*: "To God belongs both East and West. He guides whomsoever he wills into a way that is straight."

Like the young Egyptian doctor Omnia Marzouk, Berta Passweg, an older woman from Israel, was watching the ceremony on the White House lawn when Israeli and Palestinian leaders shook hands. To her, it was the source of great joy and the fulfillment of something she had been praying for and dreaming of for many years. "Whatever the problems that still exist between the

Berta Passweg at her desk in 1949 in Tel Aviv, where she was a social worker for twenty years. Photograph from the Passweg collection.

Jewish population and the Arab neighbors in and outside our frontiers," she says, "my heart remains open for the Arabs, and strong is my hope for peace and cooperation."

Like many other older Jews, she has lived through the horrors of this century: the loss of family members, the uprooting from community, the need again and again to overcome a feeling of being unwelcome. Yet, far from giving any sense of bitterness or frustration over what she has had to undergo, she reflects an optimism that the future can be different.

Berta was born in Poland in 1911. In 1914, when the Cossack pogroms began, the family escaped to Vienna. Some time afterward, they were led to believe that all was quiet and they returned. But in 1916, as the pogroms restarted, they set off for Vienna again in cold, wet, drafty cattle cars. This time they stayed.

Berta had dreamed of becoming a teacher, but since she had to contribute to the family income, she enrolled in a business school. At age seventeen, she began working as a secretary in an export-import firm, eventually becoming secretary to the boss, who was also Jewish. Sensing the impending danger as Hitler consolidated his power, the owners transferred part of the enterprise to Egypt, which was then a British protectorate. Berta's one sister had left earlier for Palestine.

Following the *Anschluss*, the German annexation of Austria in 1938, Berta was able to join this Cairo branch, hoping that the other members of her family would be able to get out too. Her father had died by then, so the family members who were still in Austria met to decide what to do. Most agreed that they should try to escape. One brother managed to live through the war by hiding out in Austria; another brother disappeared, last seen heading for Hungary. The sister who was living in Palestine applied to the British authorities for a visa for her mother. It did not arrive in time, and the mother died in Auschwitz. The boss of the company was also sent to a concentration camp.

With the outbreak of war in 1939, Berta looked for a way to help the Allied armies. She started taking evening courses on first aid from the Red Cross. She also gave German lessons. Her old firm had transferred to the United States, so she had joined an English export-import company. Then, realizing that she needed a better-paying job, she applied for and was accepted for the Anglo-Egyptian censorship. Later she attended the school for social work, L'École Superieure du Travail Social, in Alexandria. She worked at the International Bureau for the Protection of Women and Children and in a hospital. In 1946, just after the war, she got more practical experience in an institution for difficult boys in Albisbrunn, Switzerland. For five years she worked at the Social Center in Alexandria.

During her life in Egypt, Berta laid many of the moral foundations of her life. When she was at the English export-import firm, for instance, she decided that she would no longer use the company stationery for her private letters, would reimburse the company for private use of the telephone, and, as she informed her boss, not say that he was out if he was in but say that he was busy. Later she saw evidence of her boss's positive reaction when he asked her to take responsibility for the office in his absence. She also began to consciously work with people of different communities anddifferent faiths and to find the common ground on which they could unite. She learned to be responsible and not to regard herself as a refugee.

During the war, a friend in Alexandria said to her, "Berta, you should pray for Hitler." Her first reaction, as she contemplated the horrors of Europe and what had happened to her family, was that her friend was crazy. But her friend said, "I don't mean you to pray that he succeeds with his evil intentions, but that God changes his mind."

"It took me some time until I was ready to do it, but finally I did," she says. "I don't think it had any effect on Hitler, but it had an effect on me: I felt that all hate and bitterness against the Germans had just vanished and I could later meet and talk with Germans without any resentment."

With the postwar changes in the Middle East, particularly the creation of the Jewish state, life became more difficult for Jews in Egypt, and in 1951, Berta left for Vienna. A year later, she settled in Israel, where she began her work with the Social Service Department of Tel Aviv. In 1972, she retired after twenty years of social work in Tel Aviv and has continued in her efforts to encourage people of different backgrounds to work together. She has regularly attended the Caux conference, starting in its first year, 1946. There she works quietly behind the scenes.

One evening in Caux in 1993, the great meeting hall was cleared for a communal prayer in the round. Hundreds gathered in a circle under the dome of what was once the main hall of the Caux Palace Hotel. The younger ones sat on the floor. Children came with baskets of flowers. In the center of the room was a small round table with a large candle, and around it were many small candles. There was extraordinary variety in the expression of the search for God.

Music ranged from a Bach chorale, "Jesu, Joy of Man's Desiring," to a guitar meditation on Aboriginal "deep listening," to a Swahili hymn. In between were periods of silence. Everyone joined in singing "Amazing Grace." Prayers of adoration, confession, and intercession were offered from different faiths and continents— some formal centuries-old prayers, some more simple modern expressions of need. An Indian scholar led a *Bhajan*, a Muslim

Palestinian read from the Qur'ān, a Thai gave a Buddhist chant. There were prayers for healing, for people divided by barriers, for the courage to be faithful, for leaders of different countries, for those with disabilities; there were spontaneous prayers from the men and women and children from some fifty countries.

Berta offered the second prayer that night, a prayer in Hebrew that she says every night: "Hear, oh Israel, the Lord our God is One. Blessed be thy name for his glorious kingdom for ever and ever. You shall love the Lord your God with all your heart, with all your soul, and with all your mind. And the words which I command you today shall be in your heart. You shall impress them on your children and you shall speak of them when you are at home, when you are on a journey, when you lay down, and when you rise up. And you shall write them on the doorpost of your house and your gate."

"Nobody moved, not even the children, there was an indescribable atmosphere of holiness," she said. "I felt spellbound." To her it was a portent of how this center of reconciliation might be used in the future to bring together people from different sides to further the peace process in the Middle East. "I never experienced such an evening before," she says.

14

FROM VISION TO ACTION

"AGNES, THERE IS SOMETHING I have never told you that I think you ought to know. I was one of the committee in the Mau Mau that chose your father to be a sacrifice and planned his death."

Stanley Kinga's quiet words over dinner in the Caux dining room were a shock to Agnes Hofmeyr, a white Kenyan who now lives in South Africa. She could hardly believe her ears, and she asked him to repeat them. He did so. Then she said, "Thank God we have both learned the secret of forgiveness or we could never sit here."

It took courage on the part of this former leader of the Mau Mau, an extreme wing of the Kenyan independence movement, to admit that he had had a part in the death of a much-respected white settler and on the part of Agnes to accept his words with such grace. Singled out as a good white man whose death might advance the prospects of the Mau Mau, her father had been buried alive. For Agnes, who had been working to improve race relations, it was a shattering blow. But she had a clear thought, which she believed came from God: "Have no bitterness or hatred but fight harder than ever to bring a change of heart to black and white alike." She obeyed that thought and went even further, facing up to the fact that whites needed forgiveness for the way they had treated blacks.

For many years, Agnes and her husband, Bremer, worked for racial unity in South Africa, often in the face of strong criticism from other whites. They pioneered interracial conferences long before these became normal. So she was ready for that dinner and could welcome Stanley's next words: "There is something more I want you to know. Recently I was part of a committee to nominate candidates to represent KANU [the government party] at the general election. I got your cousin, Philip Leakey, nominated as the candidate for an entirely black constituency. He was elected, and today he is the only white member of our Parliament. In fact, he is now a junior minister."

A conference session the next day was set to deal with forgiveness, and it was suggested that the two speak together as evidence of the unity that can come even between the most divided through a change of heart. Agnes hesitated; her sister-in-law was at the conference. Would she understand? "Of course you must do it," her sister-in-law said. "This is what the world needs to know—the answer to hatred and bitterness."

Forgiveness and the answer to bitterness are a common element at the heart of the experiences of many of the women in this book. They have decided to move beyond blame and to deal with Ma Mi's "three fingers pointing back at me": Irene Laure asking the Germans for forgiveness for her hatred; Renee Pan reaching out to the Khmer Rouge, who had murdered her family; Shidzue Kato apologizing to the Filipinos and Koreans for what Japan had done in World War II; Alice Wedega willing to give the Australians another chance.

Another common element is courage—courage in the face of death or in the face of ridicule, the courage to buck tradition or depart from the accepted way, the courage to stand alone: Saidie Patterson confronting her employer; Abeba Tesfagiorgis standing unflinching in front of the firing squad; Sushobha Barve choosing to live in the middle of the Bombay riots. Another woman of supreme courage is Irina Ratushinskaya, one of the initiators of the 1994 Creators of Peace session. The Russian poet and author was sentenced to seven years in a Soviet labor camp, the longest sentence for a political crime imposed on any woman since the days of Stalin. She says, "If you start to hate you can never stop. To hold on to your personality, to survive, even to keep your common sense, you have to kill hatred immediately."

The women in this book would, I believe, agree with that perspective, believing that peacemaking in the world begins with a quality of peace in one's own life. Harmony between family and professional commitments was the plea of the Reverend Dr. Ella Mitchell, one of the first women ordained in the American Baptist church, when she spoke at the 1991 Creators of Peace session. "People change best in peaceful communication," she said. She had quietly moved around and through the traditional barriers set against women. "I have lived to see far more change with my strategy than I have ever seen with shouting matches and acrimonious encounters."

In many of these women there is also a component of faith and a sense of the importance of perspective, of taking time to step back and be quiet. They would surely agree with the Dalai Lama, who said at Caux, "The world peace we urgently need can be achieved through mental peace." And they would agree with Mother Teresa, who was awarded the Nobel Peace Prize in 1979 and said that in order to pray for peace there must first be the ability to listen: "We must have the courage and the time to listen to the word of God. As long as we are not able to hear God's voice when he speaks in the silence of the heart, we will not be able to pray or express our love in action."

Madame Helene Guisan-Demetriades, one of the Swiss who has worked to make the continuation of the Caux conferences possible, spoke there in 1993 and said that the deepest thing she had discovered at Caux thirty years earlier was the concept of a daily time of quiet. In fact, she calls a day without a time of silent reflection "a day where one is blind." It is not a time of emptying the mind totally, she says, but rather a place of rich creative thought, an hour of solitude and peace when one is freed of stress, away from activity of all kinds. During such times, we can welcome the thoughts that would not visit us if we were not withdrawn from the hustle and bustle of life. To avoid being invaded by all the cares, preoccupations, and problems of the previous day, the cries of our own desires, fears, bitterness, and anguish, she recommends "taking the elevator," which she describes as "opening the Bible or some other book of wisdom and truth that lifts our spirit and carries us above our ordinary level of thought."

Dr. Charis Waddy confirms that this approach is a uniting element between people of different faiths. As a Christian, she has used her life to do just that. She was the first woman to study Arabic at Oxford and wrote her thesis on the Arab side of the Crusades. Her books, including *The Muslim Mind*, have forged respect for the truths of the Muslim world and made them real for thousands of non-Muslims. If communities and nations are to live at peace, she says, they have to find a way to work with those who have different cultural, religious, and racial backgrounds and opinions. And that begins with individuals finding a source of direction in their lives. She spoke at a 1977 session at Caux on "The Skills of Discernment" and outlined the daily discipline that is common to most of the people described in this book: "The experience of the inner voice, of the guidance of God, is an area of personal experiment in which each individual is privileged to find his or her own way. No one can hear God's word in their heart for you. My own experience over the past forty years has been of a very ordinary nature. It has centered in the use of that unemotional hour in the morning when, like it or not, come wind come weather, one has to get up. No tongues of flame, no flashing lights, no ecstasies: the cooling and redirection of passion, rather than the rousing of it. I have lived a normal and in many ways a very ordinary life, with personally little of the dramatic or traumatic to report. Perhaps the normality of the sense of inner direction that has accompanied it is the notable point.

"Through all the varied conflicts of these years, I can say that the inner experiences of God's guidance, and the pattern of life it represents, have made sense. In air raid shelters and food shortages, in company and in isolation, in professional work and household chores, in the humdrum and the hair-raising, the way of life that I chose when I was twenty-two has proved to be valid. It has never been easy, but it has worked. In my own experience and that of others, it has a good record of durability in the harsh tests to which the turbulence of the twentieth century has put it."

The women in this book have not been content just to take on a local situation or address only one issue. As they have demonstrated in their lives, they have been willing to take on the world. Although for each there was an element of standing alone, for most there was also the aspect of doing it together with others.

"From Vision to Action" was the theme of a 1994 Caux conference session. Joan Holland, a retired headmistress of a school in Auckland, New Zealand, envisages women moving together into areas of crisis and bringing their particular qualities to bear. She says that women develop a natural creativity within the home and need to put their imagination and gifts to work on a wider level. "We share so much of life, we have a gentler quality, some of us. We're people-centered, no doubt about it. We're more concerned with individuals than with broader plans. As women we naturally respond to each other with more heart."

Claire Evans, a Frenchwoman who often translated for Madame Laure, wrote in her book *Freewoman*:

There is a price to pay in applying radical solutions; it is change in our nature. We can accept it or refuse it. There are moments of choice. When a friend offers me a truth about myself, or an enemy throws one full in my face, when I see something amiss under the surface in someone else's life, or begin to feel that things around me are going awry, I have two options. I can either turn my back on the truth and try to go on as before, or look straight at the truth and change. All our human resources of clarity and courage are not enough, you will say. But who is stopping us from appealing to divine resources? And if we are bent on competing with the men, we can always show that we accept change quicker than they! The road which is opened up by this possibility of radical change is not a theoretical road, but one which leads through the rough and the smooth of our daily lives. (p. 41)

Many of the women in this book have remarkable stories. That is, of course, why they were told. Behind the scenes are other women whose stories may be less dramatic but no less costly, and there are younger women who are starting to make a difference around them. The Reverend Paige Chargois from Richmond, Virginia, who is coordinating Creators of Peace globally, says, "It gives me hope to see a cornucopia of women becoming public peacemakers and bold advocates even in some of the most frightful conditions in our world's cities, simply following in the footsteps of their historical mothers."

APPENDIX

MOUNTAIN HOUSE, THE FORMER Caux Palace Hotel, was bought in 1946 by a group of Swiss. Their country had been spared the ravages of World War II, and they wanted to provide a center where the hurts and hates of that war could be healed. They were associated with Moral Re-Armament (MRA), a worldwide organization working for change and reconciliation initiated by American Frank Buchman. (Called the Oxford Group in the 1930s, its best-known spinoff is Alcoholics Anonymous.)

Buchman's first question when he arrived at the opening of the center was, "Where are the Germans?" This question set in motion a process that brought together thousands of Germans and French and helped lay the basis for the new Europe.

The French daily *Le Monde* (July 20, 1988), wrote that at Caux "a thousand and one links have been forged in a kind of parallel diplomacy, apparently unstructured, which counts on the human heart rather than on the weight of arms to resolve conflicts and bring the world closer together."

Over the years, Caux has hosted thousands of remarkable

women from every continent. They have found, in its spectacular setting three thousand feet above Lake Geneva, in its spacious and restful atmosphere, in its openness to people of all backgrounds, and in its emphasis on responsibility rather than blame, a place where their deepest convictions can find expression. As the great American singer Marian Anderson said, "The inspiring days I spent at this beautiful and sacred spot will remain a treasured memory. I never knew that there was a vast army of people of so many races pledged to put right what is wrong in the world."

The women in this book have found inspiration and support for their work at Caux.

BIBLIOGRAPHY

Allen, Leonard, and Kathleen Allen. *People, Pagodas and Pyramids*. Stamford, CT, 1985.

Bleakley, David. *Saidie Patterson, Irish Peacemaker*. Belfast: Blackstaff, 1980.

Center for Strategic and International Studies. *Religion, The Missing Dimension of Statecraft*. New York: Oxford University Press, 1994.

Connell, Dan. *Against All Odds*. Trenton, NJ: Red Sea Press, 1993.

Davidson, Basil. *African Civilization Revisited*. Trenton, NJ: Red Sea Press, 1990.

Entwistle, Basil. *Japan's Decisive Decade*. London: Grosvenor, 1985.

Evans, Claire. *Freewoman*. Oxford: Becket Publications, 1979.

Hamlin, Bryan. *Forgiveness in International Affairs*. London: Grosvenor, 1992.

Hofmeyr, Agnes. *Beyond Violence*. Johannesburg: Grosvenor, 1990.

Ishimoto, Shidzue. *Facing Two Ways* [1935]. Stanford: Stanford University Press, 1984.

Keneally, Thomas. *Schindler's List.* New York: Simon and Schuster, 1982.

Lean, Garth. *On the Tail of a Comet.* Colorado Springs: Helmers and Howard, 1988.

Mackay, Malcolm. *More Than Coincidence.* Edinburgh: Saint Andrew Press, 1979.

Menchú, Rigoberta. *I, Rigoberta Menchú: An Indian Woman in Guatemala.* New York: Verso, 1983.

Mowat, Robin. *Decline and Renewal.* Oxford: New Cherwell Press, 1991.

Piguet, Jacqueline. *For the Love of Tomorrow.* London: Grosvenor 1986.

Procter, Marjorie. *The World My Country.* London: Grosvenor, 1976.

Sena, Surya. *Of Sri Lanka I Sing.* Colombo: Ranco Publishers, 1978.

Sherrard, Mary S., ed. *Women of Faith.* Edinburgh: Saint Andrew Press, 1993.

Tesfagiorgis, Abeba. *A Painful Season and a Stubborn Hope.* Trenton, NJ: Red Sea Press, 1992.

Twitchell, Kenaston. *Regeneration in the Ruhr.* Princeton, NJ: Princeton University Press, 1981.

Tyndale-Biscoe, John. *For God Alone.* Oxford: Amate Press, 1984.

Vaughan, Berkeley. *Doctor in Papua.* Edinburgh: Saint Andrew Press, 1974.

Waddy, Charis. *The Muslim Mind.* London/New York: Longman, 1976.

Waddy, Charis. *The Skills of Discernment.* London: Grosvenor, 1977.

Wedega, Alice. *Listen, My Country.* Sydney: Pacific Publications, 1981.

West, G. *The World That Works.* Bombay: Thacker, n.d.

ABOUT THE AUTHOR

Born in England, Michael Henderson is a freelance journalist, author, and commentator on public radio stations in Oregon. He is a recipient of national and local awards for his radio commentaries and newspapers columns. His articles have appeared in numerous daily newspapers including the *Christian Science Monitor,* the *Oregonian,* the *St. Louis Dispatch,* the *Baltimore Sun,* and the *Orange County Register.* He is also the author of five books, most recently *Hope for a Change: Commentaries by an Optimistic Realist.*